The
Cheat
Sheet

Foreword by TOMMY HABEEB,
former writer, producer, and host of *Cheaters*

The Cheat Sheet

A Clue-by-Clue Guide to Finding Out If He's Unfaithful

REA FREY &
STEPHANY ALEXANDER,
founder of WomanSavers.com

adamsmedia
Avon, Massachusetts

Published by
Adams Media, a division of F+W Media, Inc.
57 Littlefield Street, Avon, MA 02322. U.S.A.
www.adamsmedia.com

ISBN 10: 1-4405-1198-5
ISBN 13: 978-1-4405-1198-1
eISBN 10: 1-4405-1434-8
eISBN 13: 978-1-4405-1434-0

Printed in the United States of America.

10   9   8   7   6   5   4   3   2   1

Library of Congress Cataloging-in-Publication Data
Frey, Rea.
The cheat sheet / Rea Frey and Stephany Alexander.
p. cm.
ISBN-13: 978-1-4405-1198-1
ISBN-10: 1-4405-1198-5
ISBN-13: 978-1-4405-1434-0 (ebk)
ISBN-10: 1-4405-1434-8 (ebk)
1. Men—Sexual behavior. 2. Men—Psychology. 3. Man-woman relationships. I. Alexander,
Stephany. II. Title.
HQ28.F74 2011
306.7081—dc22
2011008861

This book is available at quantity discounts for bulk purchases.
For information, please call 1-800-289-0963.

To all of the couples who are building a house:
Remember that love is the foundation,
sex is the exterior,
friendship is the interior,
and a sense of humor is everything else
when the house comes tumbling down.

Contents

Foreword ix

Acknowledgments xi

Introduction. xiii

Chapter 1. "It Just Happened" 1

Chapter 2. "A Cheating Culture" 9

Chapter 3. "It's Physical". 21

Chapter 4. "It's Emotional". 33

Chapter 5. "It's In My DNA" 45

Chapter 6. "People Lack Discipline" 65

Chapter 7. "Workplace Affairs". 89

Chapter 8. "Online Affairs". 99

Chapter 9. "Worst-Case Scenarios" 109

Chapter 10. "Picking Up the Pieces" 119

Chapter 11. "Making Your Relationship Affair-Proof" 137

Appendix A. Resources 163

Appendix B. Extras: Cheat-Sheet Tales 167

Index 213

Foreword

As a former host to one of the most popular infidelity shows, *Cheaters*, I have seen my fair share of heartbreak. I've seen the mistakes, the humility, and the pain people go through because of affairs. So, how do we deal with this unfortunate part of relationships? In *The Cheat Sheet*, Ms. Frey and Ms. Alexander delve into this subject matter with full force, wit, and refreshing honesty. Both experts in their own rights, they lay it out: If you think your partner might be cheating on you, they will show you every clue to look for. They will give you tools, a gadget guide, and stellar advice on how to deal with infidelity and how to "affair-proof" your relationships.

The authors manage to draw the reader into the secret lives of philanderers by giving firsthand accounts of cheating stories. The reader discovers how cheaters justify their acts, handle guilt, cope with double lives, and handle the search for commitment and outside gratification. There are important "tips of the trade," valuable to both women and men. *The Cheat Sheet* is an excellent how-to guide to prevent and uncover cheating—every woman's secret weapon.

As Ariana Huffington put it, texting is the new lipstick on the collar. Let's prevent these marks. Let's catch cheaters, learn to think before we act, and perhaps we can better understand and attempt that ten-letter word we have become so frightened of: commitment.

—TOMMY HABEEB

Actor/Writer/Producer and Host of the TV Show *Cheaters*

Acknowledgments

The authors would first like to thank the human race and the complexities of love, for without either of these, there would be no need for a book like this; Serendipity Literary Agency, for taking a chance on a difficult but timely subject matter and its very diverse authors; the amazing guidance and effort of Foladé Bell; Adams Media for their steadfast loyalty and support with this book; and Victoria Sandbrook and Jennifer Lawler, editors extraordinaire.

Rea would also like to thank the alphabet; her father for teaching her that alphabet; and Alex, for bringing her true love after a lifetime of imposters. Stephany would like to thank her friends and family who have stuck by her through thick and thin; and the amazing man in her life, David, who restored her faith in men.

Introduction

We've all heard stories of cheating. From personal tragedies to high-profile celebrity public disgraces, cheating has reached epidemic proportions. Infidelity is widespread, and it is a serious issue in many relationships today. If your partner is cheating (or you suspect he is), you've come to the right place. This book is intended to help you uncover every clue of infidelity, show you what to do if you discover infidelity, and how to prevent affairs from ever happening. If you want to catch a cheater, you must understand why and how someone cheats: what he's thinking and how he gets away with it. This book is full of signs, tips, tools, and quizzes for those who are or may be dealing with an unfaithful partner.

As authors, we've seen our fair share of cheating. Rea spent a year entrenched in the lies and secrets of an affair before realizing that her lover wasn't *actually* going to leave his wife. She now understands firsthand the havoc infidelity can wreak and is committed to helping others through that heartache. Stephany founded Woman Savers.com Date Screening Service, a website devoted to giving women a way to research and rate the men in their lives, so they can make smarter and safer dating decisions. Together, we have an unbeatable perspective on what cheaters think they can get away with and how you can find out if your partner is cheating on you.

No matter how "well" an affair is handled by everyone involved, everyone gets hurt. A relationship that includes infidelity isn't a *relationship*. Relationships don't result in seedy hotels, cash-only bills, erased text messages and secret meetings. If a person is cheating, he isn't living in reality; he's living in a hurtful fantasy. That being said, affairs happen every day and if you have suspicions that your partner is being unfaithful, you're right to worry. It is best to arm yourself with the necessary tools to catch a cheating partner and learn how to prevent this act entirely.

In the book, we're assuming you're a woman worried about her male partner cheating, but women and men do cheat on each other in approximately the same numbers, and same-sex couples aren't immune. The information we give is true and accurate regardless of whether you or your partner is male or female.

Let's start with some of the most common signs a partner is cheating:

SIGNS YOUR PARTNER IS CHEATING

- Suddenly starts working late
- Turns off a cell phone or leaves the room when taking a call
- Keeps a password you don't know on his cell phone
- Takes sudden business trips or is gone for unexplained periods of time
- Unusual, out-of-character behavior changes or sudden gift giving
- Goes out more
- Gets defensive when questioned
- Turns phone away when texting so you can't see the screen
- Unaccounted-for hairs of a different color on clothing
- Dresses up more, changes physical appearance, starts wearing cologne, or asks you to change your appearance

- Stays on the computer for hours and gets jumpy when you enter the room
- Sets computer up to erase history (cache) or erases it manually
- Car radio station is switched to a station different from what either of you listen to
- Passenger seat in the car has been moved and is not in the usual position
- Unexplained cash withdrawals from ATM
- More cash is being spent with no receipts
- Low on cash
- Long phone calls to unexplained numbers
- Brings up a new person in random conversation repeatedly
- Car mileage suddenly goes up
- Discovery of a P.O. Box
- Cigarette smoke or perfume on clothing that can't be explained
- Secretion stains on underwear

CHEAT-SHEET TIP

If your radar goes up, listen to your intuition. People are usually very in tune with their feelings. Confirming your hunch isn't that hard in this tech-savvy world. Luckily, a few new gadgets have come out to track a cheating partner (see Chapter 6, the section entitled "Cheating Gadget Guide"). According to Guy White, a private investigator, you can install devices on your phone to record conversations, and on your computer to check e-mails. Arm yourself. Don't have the money for gadgets? Buy a wig, some glasses, grab a friend to help you, and follow the suspect. Become your own Nancy Drew. It's liberating.

WHO CHEATS?

Though cheating statistics are hard to obtain (since many people will not fess up to the act), the consensus is absolute (according to *www.menstuff.org*): about 50 percent of both women and men cheat on their spouses or significant others.

Stay-at-home parents, executives, writers, artists, scholars, doctors, nurses, journalists, detectives, clergy, politicians, lawyers, and even teens cheat. It crosses gender, professions, age, and ethnicity. According to a poll at WomanSavers.com, African-American women complain the most about cheating partners, and people between the ages of eighteen and sixty cheat the most.

WHAT IS CHEATING?

Before you start dissecting your partner's actions, you have to decide what really defines cheating. Is there a difference to you between emotional, mental, and physical cheating? Does kissing count as cheating? Telling someone he has feelings for her? Meeting in secret? A little heavy petting? Online flirting? Sex? Full-blown affairs? What about fantasizing? Is that cheating? Is looking at pornography cheating? Is sexting (sexually texting) someone other than you cheating? Is confiding his innermost secrets and feelings to someone of the opposite sex or someone he *could* be sexually attracted to cheating? What actually constitutes infidelity in your relationship?

Some women may have no problem with viewing pornography, while others may find it offensive and upsetting, especially if viewing pornography takes his mind away from intimacy with you, his real-life partner. What about fantasizing about someone other than you while having sex? Does it make a difference to you if the fantasy is about someone you know versus someone unattainable, like a celebrity? Is there ever an excuse valid enough to condone cheating? To be unfaithful? By discussing some of these questions with your partner, his answers may reveal hidden feelings and actions he thought were harmless or innocent. Like most things, infidelity is not as cut-and-dried as it seems.

In this book, we will discuss all angles of affairs, from that first inkling that something is going on, to every tip, tool, and trick to catching a partner, reconnecting with a partner, leaving a partner, or staying with a partner despite infidelity. Use *The Cheat Sheet* as your survival guide. Tell your friends, and warn your partners. It's all here: the good, the bad, and the tricky aspects of cheating and surviving infidelity. Happy sleuthing!

CHAPTER ONE

"It Just Happened"

"Love is a game in which one always cheats."

—HONORÉ DE BALZAC (FRENCH NOVELIST)

FALLING INTO ADULTERY

I rolled over and lit a cigarette—it would be my last shared with Luke. I looked at his elbow, slightly ashy, and laughed. "Lotion," I said, a plume of smoke disappearing towards the ceiling. "You need lotion."

He turned to look at me, already having slipped his wedding band back on. "And you need a conscience," he said. He kissed me on the cheek and left. I counted his footsteps down my stairs and rolled over in my marital bed. I wasn't sure what I had become, and why I didn't seem to be peppered with guilt about having an affair. Three months ago, I was in a shitty marriage, and then, Luke had "just happened," literally appearing out of thin air.

I wasn't the kind of woman who just met people. I was quiet, cynical even, a painter who did well enough and had a husband who made too much money for a job he couldn't stand. I was bored. At the farmer's market, Luke and I fought over the same batch of heirloom tomatoes.

1

We went for coffee. He took my hand at the end of our time together and pressed his lips to my wedding ring.

"A shame," he said, buffing it with a handkerchief he pulled from his jacket pocket.

"Why do you have a handkerchief? Who has handkerchiefs anymore? And besides," I said, shoving my hand in my pocket, "you have one too."

"One what?" He cocked his head to the side like a small dog who'd just heard some strange noise.

"A wedding ring."

"Aren't you observant," he said.

A week later, we were in bed. I don't know how. It literally just happened. *I let it* just happen *for three months. I lied to my husband about where I was and who I was with, and as soon as he left for work, I called Luke, who would stop whatever he was doing and rush right over to ravage me. After weeks of betrayal, I couldn't do it anymore. I broke it off and never saw him again, my husband none the wiser.*

I figured out what I needed in my marriage was a closeness and intimacy that we had lost over the years. I wanted a friend. I wanted to be appreciated. I didn't like what my marriage had become.

And so I confessed my sin to my husband over pasta on a random Wednesday. He looked up from his plate of capellini, a glob of tomato sauce glued to his chin.

"Like an affair *affair?" he asked. "When?"*

I shrugged. "It was a few months back. He wasn't anybody special."

My husband was calm, so calm that it unnerved me. "Have you had one too?" I asked. He shifted uncomfortably in his chair, which told me yes. Oddly, I felt relieved. Oddly, I felt normal and connected to him in a way that I hadn't in years. Because of our admissions, we worked it out. We went to therapy—something I had always rejected—

and worked through our issues. Through brutal honesty, endless hours of communication, and ample willingness, we have found our way to happiness again.

HOW CHEATERS GET AWAY WITH CHEATING

Cheaters often talk about how the affair "just happened." But in many cases, a lot of planning goes into cheating. The entire concept of cheating is based on secrecy. To lie and deceive, there has to be forethought and planning that goes into each and every action. Your partner can't just stumble in at midnight and say, "I was out with the boys," and expect you to believe him. Cheaters come up with proper alibis, excuses, and often cover their tracks by erasing all the evidence.

You may think your partner isn't having an affair just because he doesn't leave any obvious clues around. But you may be surprised to learn what is actually a clue. The most common clues are left around the house, or can be found simply in the way his behavior patterns change. If you have that gut feeling your partner could be straying, look for the following traces of infidelity:

1. Perfume: If he just bought you a new perfume, it could be because it's the same perfume his new lover uses. By using the same scent, you won't be suspicious if you smell it on him. If he did buy you a new perfume, tell him you love it, but don't wear it. See if you can smell a different scent on him, which is a strong clue that he is cheating.

2. Paper Trail: If you are curious as to what he's been buying, check his credit card statements. These might be online (check his e-mail) or search in a filing cabinet. If the bills don't have any unusual items or charges, he could be using cash to pay for everything, so pay attention to unexplained ATM withdrawals, or if he is cashing his checks instead of depositing them. Question him about his spending or propose that you would like to sit down and go over your financials and get on more of a budget. You might even offer to take care of the finances completely. If he seems resistant to this or is very secretive about his bills or money, this could be a sign of infidelity.

3. *Alibis:* Cheaters often have friends who will vouch for them. If he's going out, he usually doesn't get dressed up, since he is just hanging out with a friend. (This would be a good time to check his trunk for an extra pair of clothing.) If he tells you he's going someplace, don't take it at face value if you're suspicious. Question him before he goes out and after he returns. Most cheaters will be able to explain where they were, but if your partner seems nervous or defensive, probe a little deeper. For example, most cheaters don't make stupid excuses like, "I'm going to do laundry" at 10:00 P.M. just to get out of the house. They tend to make excuses that serve their partner in some way. If he has to run out, it will be for a believable reason. He might offer to put gas in your car to save you a trip in the morning. While you are reveling in his generosity, he could be taking the chance to call his lover or meet up with her. On his way home from work, he could offer to pick up groceries and then choose to swing by her place first (or even meet her *at* the store). If he comes in the door later than usual, he could explain he got caught in traffic and there was a crazy line at the grocery store.

4. *Phone:* Look for clues when he's on the phone. It might seem like he's just talking to a friend (if he's talking to someone in front

of you), but he might have a code that he and his lover are speaking in. He might be talking to a very important "client" about setting up a business meeting and needs to have privacy while on the phone, so he goes into another room. He could call her by a different name, no name, or even a friend's name. Lovers speak in code all the time, and the more normal he appears, the easier it is for him to get away with deception.

5. *Behavior:* If your partner is cheating and is discreet about his affairs, he's going to be careful not to treat you differently in terms of sex, his level of interest in you, and conversations he has with you. He knows that if his behavior changes, it will be a red flag that something is going on. If a cheater starts showing signs of cheating, such as losing interest in you, or staying late "at work," he'll avoid your questions, telling you he's stressed, or turn the problem back on you. Cheaters are masters at deflecting questions and making you feel crazy.

A very defensive partner can be a clue, as can an overly affectionate partner (when the affection comes out of the blue). If you complain that you haven't been having sex lately, he might blame that on you, saying you never initiate sex. He might make you feel guilty by saying he's incredibly overworked and feels too much pressure when he's at home. He can make you feel selfish and needy, when in fact he is the one who is acting in betrayal. It's a common desire for men to have the comfort of their relationships while fulfilling their other desires. It is a justification of many cheaters and often allows your partner to maintain his double life.

6. *Details:* Cheaters can give just enough details that contain a portion of the truth to throw you off track. For example, he might

casually mention the name of a female coworker he is working on a project with, when in fact she could be in a different department entirely. He could mention his female friend who is married, when in fact she is single or separated. He could talk about his new lesbian friend, when she's not really a lesbian. He knows what to talk about and what details to reveal to make you feel like other women aren't threats to your relationship. Cheaters know how to ease your suspicions by revealing just enough of the details to placate your curiosity without revealing the entire truth. They also pay attention to physical details. They check their clothing for stains or rips—anything that might give away what they've been up to. They always wear the same clothes they left in and are also smart enough to stick to their daily routine. His odometer probably isn't going to show he traveled 500 miles today when he's claiming he just drove to the grocery store and back. He'll adjust the odometer (or the story) so as not to rouse suspicion.

SURVIVAL-GUIDE TOOL
POSSIBLE HIDDEN CLUES IN THE HOME

If you suspect your partner is cheating, search your home (and his, if you live separately) for clues. Use the following guide as a starting point to locate and collect evidence of possible infidelity:

- Hairs on sheets, clothing, or in sinks and drains
- Bobby pins or rubber bands on floors*
- Mementos stuffed in gym bags, filing cabinets, or briefcases
- Raunchy photos hidden in other "normal" magazines
- Receipts in purses or wallets

- Journals or photographs in nightstands
- Extra jewelry or mementos stashed in jewelry boxes
- Hidden letters crammed into books
- Condom wrappers or "used" paper towels in the garbage, especially in the bathroom or kitchen
- Secret letters in unassuming file names on the desktop or in a Word document (search by looking for the most recent dates)
- Instant messenger chat history
- Cell phone texts, voice mails, pictures, and call logs

Though bobby pins or extra rubber bands on floors might not seem like a big deal, you know what's yours and what isn't. These are often the clues that can reveal affairs—subtle clues. Pay attention to what is in your home, car, dresser, bags, and bathrooms.

UNCOVER

HOW CHEATERS HIDE SIGNS OF CHEATING

You've checked the bathroom for hairs that don't belong to you and the bedroom for signs that he's been sleeping with someone else while you were out of town. You've checked bank statements, his car, filing cabinets, his desk, computer, and phone. And you've come up empty. You may think, "Sure, cheaters are careful to get the details right, but no one can be perfect. So maybe he's not cheating?"

You'd be surprised. If he's cheating at home, there are usually clues. Take a photo of the bedroom or the room in question before you leave for the day. While a cheater will try to cover his tracks by making sure he puts everything back (washing the sheets, making the bed, and vacuuming), he is bound to miss something.

Plant a small piece of paper, a rubber band, or something unobtrusive beneath the sheets or a pillowcase to see if it has been moved when you return home. You can also make the bed a certain way (a way only you know how to do) so that you might uncover whether the bed was used and then remade while you were away. When you return home, also check wastebaskets and drains (for hair, used paper towels, or wrapped-up condoms).

If you both have a job outside of the home, pretend you are going to work and then secretly take the day off (or even come home for lunch). While he's gone, comb every single part of the house, making sure to put things back in order. Search the computer—every Word document, every file name, and the computer's history to see what you can come up with. Check the drains, the cabinets, the trash cans, bags, closets, attics, whatever you can get your hands on. Stay calm and refrain from tearing the house end from end, but do search thoroughly.

For many sneaky cheaters, they will hide a lot of the evidence at work. Keep this in mind and perhaps drop in on your spouse one day while he's out to lunch. Search his office if you have a moment alone, focusing on his computer and any voice mails he might have. Check the computer's history, as he probably won't be proactive about clearing his history at work.

Covering all of your tracks while really searching your home or his office is the first step to busting an unfaithful partner.

CHAPTER TWO

"A Cheating Culture"

"Eighty percent of married men cheat in America.
The rest cheat in Europe."

—JACKIE MASON (AMERICAN COMEDIAN)

CHEAT-SHEET TALE
ADDICTED TO ADULTERY

Everyone has an addiction. For some, it's jumping out of planes. For others, it's volunteering—it gives them a purpose that can't be found in day-to-day life. For me, that high, that adrenaline rush, that purpose can only emerge from the knobby spine of a bare-backed woman, the uneven skin of an ankle bone, or the swollen lips and breasts of a female who is not my wife.

To me, cheating is like breathing. I can cheat, go home, kiss my wife, and sleep like a baby. It gives me something to look forward to amidst the minutiae of my day. It lets me use my imagination, that creative power that remained dormant since my early days in elementary school, when glue and glitter and colored paper were strewn about a table and I felt like some genius artist constructing the next great thing. You knew your parents would love your creation, that your art would hang on your refrigerator under a heavy magnet, and that you were bringing happiness to your family in some way. Cheating has become my hidden art, leaving no traces of what I've done or where I've been.

I don't cheat because I'm a man or because it's in my DNA. I cheat because I love the feel of a woman's hair in my hands, her cheek against my cheek. I love undressing them and rubbing their backs and whispering things they have only ever dreamed about into their ear . . . and while my greatest love is reserved for my wife, my urges and impulses will always be to please all women.

I am a happy man, and I am unapologetic for what I do. I am not insecure. I don't have mommy issues. I am not heartless, and I would do anything for my wife. Perhaps, at this very moment, she is doing some version of the same thing to me, because I believe all of us have our secrets.

SOCIETY OF CHEATERS: DO ALL MEN CHEAT?

The mind of a cheater is a complex thing. They can create justifications to excuse their inappropriate behavior, no matter how hurtful, damaging, or selfish it is. While there are those rare breeds of men who have only slept with one person and are still in love, those stories are few and far between, and usually come from our grandparents' or great-grandparents' era. With the surge of the Internet, cell phones, dating sites, pornography, and endless options everywhere you look, fidelity seems pretty hard to maintain in a world of infinite choices.

How well do you know your partner? How well do you know your partner's friends? Have you hung out with them regularly in a group and observed firsthand how your partner interacts with his friends? Does he display different behavior when out with the guys as opposed to being with you? Is he a serial flirter? Have you ever discussed past relationships and how they ended? How does your partner treat women? How does he even *view* women? Is he condescending or dominating in his behavior towards other women, relatives, or you? These are all important questions and tips to note when getting to know someone. The way your partner behaves and thinks can tell you a lot about what kind of boyfriend or husband he is and what behavior you may have been ignoring. While you might be certain that he is faithful, he could be justifying his actions because that's simply the way he *thinks* in terms of relationships: having his cake and eating it too is perfectly acceptable in his mind.

"Most women who have affairs are deeply unhappy with their marriages, but it is not true of men," write David M. Buss, PhD, and Cindy M. Meston, PhD, in their book *Why Women Have Sex.* "A full 56 percent of men who have extramarital sex consider their marriages to be happy or very happy."

But that doesn't mean "He's just a guy, of course he'll cheat." *Everyone* is capable of cheating: men, women, religious people, athletes, politicians, celebrities, etc. No one is above suspicion.

Keep your eyes open and make informed decisions when choosing a partner. There's no guarantee one way or another. At the end of the day, every situation is different, and you have to talk to your partner about fidelity so you are clear about each other's viewpoints.

WHAT KIND OF CHEATER COULD HE BE?

1. What turns him on the most about someone new?
   A. Physical chemistry
   B. Sense of humor
   C. Intellectual, soulful connection
   D. All of the above

2. If he fantasizes about someone, do you think he:
   A. Imagines the person ripping his clothes off and the two of them having an unparalleled chemistry
   B. Imagines having a fun companion, someone he can laugh with and go to restaurants, bars, and movies with
   C. Imagines a woman falling in love with him, or vice versa; then the physical connection will erupt from there
   D. Wants to rip her clothes off, but he also wants to fall in love; he wants everything

3. When he's away from you, what do you think he misses the most?
   A. Your kisses, your smell, your touch
   B. How you talk and laugh about everything; you are his partner in crime, his best friend
   C. The way you look at each other, the deep conversations you have; the feeling of having a soul mate
   D. He misses your kiss, your laugh, and that feeling of true love

4. When he gives you a gift, is it usually:
   A. New lingerie
   B. Dinner and tickets to a good comedy show or play
   C. A nice bottle of wine and a book of poetry
   D. A night out on the town, followed by a bubble bath and a movie

5. If you asked your man if he could pick one trait to have in a woman, what would it be?
   A. An amazing physique
   B. Sense of humor
   C. Deeply artistic and intellectual
   D. A Renaissance woman

6. If you broke up with your man, what do you think he would miss the most?
   A. The way your bodies fit perfectly together
   B. How funny you are
   C. The romance
   D. The words, the laughter, and the insane chemistry you had

7. When you first met your partner, what was he most likely attracted to?
   A. Your looks! Hello?
   B. Your personality; you make him laugh
   C. Your intelligence and soulful quality
   D. Your humor, intelligence, and attractiveness; you had the winning combination

8. Out of the following items, which catches his eye the most?
   A. A luxury car
   B. A pair of shoes
   C. A leather journal
   D. A Rolex

9. If you ever suspected your partner of cheating, how would you find out?
   A. He smells like her
   B. He brings the other person up in conversation all the time
   C. An undeleted e-mail
   D. An overheard phone conversation

10. What do all of his ex-girlfriends have in common?
    A. They were all good-looking
    B. They always made his friends laugh
    C. They were very traditional and respectful
    D. They were the life of the party

ANSWER KEY

Mostly A's: If he was a cheater, he'd be a physical cheater. Lust is the name of the game. Physical cheaters desire and crave attention. These affairs often start out the most intense and nonsensical, because physical cheaters give in to animalistic urges. They are led by hormones, not by their brains. While relationships cannot be sustained on sex alone, one way to help make sure this type of man doesn't stray is to ensure the physical passion is still there. Find ways to connect with your partner intimately and be open to fulfilling each other's desires and fantasies.

Mostly B's: He would be a companion cheater. A companion cheater is looking for a best friend, someone who will truly be there, someone who he can befriend first. These types of affairs are dangerous, because a companion cheater will often become good friends with someone first, and then the attraction comes into play. Pay attention to who he is close friends with, and make sure he maintains proper boundaries. It's also important to make sure you maintain a friendship within your own relationship. Do you like your partner? Does your partner like you? While it's important to have intimacy, make sure you are also able to communicate and have fun together.

Mostly C's: He would be an emotional cheater. Emotional cheaters want romance and sex. They love the idea of falling for someone, or someone falling for them, even if it's just on an emotional level. They might fantasize about what could happen without acting on it. These affairs are often the messiest, because even if the attraction wanes or isn't acted upon, the emotional cheater stays connected to this person. Emotional cheaters often get caught the most, because they are sentimental and often keep mementos. In order to avoid emotional infidelity, maintain a sense of romance. Do you write each other love letters? Are you committed on an emotional level? Are you fulfilling each other's desires? Check in with each other and make sure you are both doing your part to stay connected.

Mostly D's: If he was a cheater, he'd be a combination cheater. Combo cheaters want the sex, the friendship, and the romance.

In essence, they want it all: the excitement of an affair with the comfort of a companion, all rolled into one steamy fantasy. *Fantasy* being the key word. No one can have it all, especially when it comes to an affair. Remind your partner that no relationship out there is perfect and focus on what you do have. Then discover what you could improve upon. Do you have a great friendship, but the sex is lacking? Do you have great sex, but you're not connected emotionally? Figure out ways to foster closeness in all aspects of your relationship.

UNCOVER

MOST FAMOUS MALE CHEATERS

Recently, celebrity infidelity has been surfacing everywhere, perhaps due to constant technological advances that make it harder to hide affairs. People may not be cheating *more*, but they are finally getting caught. Here's a list of the top ten most famous male cheaters in history and how these indiscretions changed, destroyed, or even enhanced their images.

1. Bill Clinton: The affair heard around the world, this is the one that perhaps most shocked and changed America, and the course of its future, due to a simple white lie: "I did not have sex with that woman." Whoever said sex and politics don't mix has obviously not heard about the numerous scandals that occur while politicians are in office. With power comes an ego, with ego comes an air of invincibility, and with invincibility comes grave mistakes, though this politician bounced back. His wife, much to the outrage of many, stood by her husband and has now cast herself in the political spotlight. And it seems to have worked: Bill is supportive, by her side, and will most likely never involve himself in another scandal again. Or, at least one where he can get caught.

2. *Jesse James:* One of the more recent scandals, but perhaps the least shocking, was that of Jesse James, who has been the quintessential bad boy. Tattooed, married twice before, in an industry that throws him in the spotlight with all types of women, it came as a great shock when he married America's Sweetheart, Sandra Bullock. People wondered what they had in common and were far from surprised when the news broke of his infidelity. Though people were still outraged, it was easy to cast him in the role of "bad boy" and her as some sort of martyr. He blamed it on not feeling "good enough" and claims to still love Sandra.

3. *Eric Benét:* In 2002, Eric Benét, a musician and Halle Berry's husband, made headlines when it was reported that he checked into a rehab facility for sex addiction after he cheated on his wife with singer Julia Riley. He blamed cheating on not being in touch with his emotions and not dealing with painful past issues. After rumors of David Duchovny's sex addiction came to light, Benét reneged on his "sex addiction" and copped up to just making a dumb mistake. The couple was purported to fight over the prenuptial agreement, but divorced in 2005.

4. *Rudy Giuliani:* The former New York City mayor has had his fair share of turbulent times (9/11, prostate cancer, and issues in his marriage). The mayor, who has been married three times, was rumored to have been unfaithful to second wife, Donna Hanover.

A bevy of ladies was said to have been "close" to the mayor, one of whom he worked with. The couple eventually divorced.

5. *John F. Kennedy:* The thirty-fifth president of the United States needs little introduction. Known for his class, poise, and style, this young president was tragically assassinated in Texas in 1963, prematurely ending his well-respected political life. His personal life, however, was up for debate. The president was said to have had affairs with Marilyn Monroe, Gunilla von Post, and Mimi Beardsley Alford.

6. *Woody Allen:* The funny director made headlines when it was discovered he was having a relationship with wife Mia Farrow's adopted daughter, Soon-Yi Previn. The affair was purportedly discovered after Mia found naked pictures of Soon-Yi in Woody's apartment. Neither the bonds of his marriage with Mia nor his thirty-four-year age difference with Soon-Yi deterred Woody, who later married Soon-Yi. To carry on their "legacy," they adopted two children of their own. Though it seemed to tarnish the director's career initially, time seems to have been an ally, as he has continued with his moviemaking career.

7. *David Letterman:* Funnyman and late-night host David Letterman, who was in a long-term relationship for many years before marrying, was the victim of a sex scandal threat, in which a CBS news employee demanded $2 million to keep quiet. Rather than pay off the person, the host confronted the allegations on live television, admitting he had slept with various women who worked on the show while in his premarital relationship. Many were outraged,

but some said it humanized him. And because he didn't lie about it, things seemed to calm down for the host, and his career has continued unaffected.

8. *Michael Jordan:* Despite being one of the greatest athletes who ever lived, Michael's life did not come without some drama on the romance front. He and his wife of sixteen years filed for divorce, then reconciled, then finally divorced shortly after, resulting in what was, at the time, the largest celebrity divorce settlement, in the form of $168 million. He entered another ugly legal battle when Karla Knafel came forward and said the ball player had promised her $5 million to keep quiet about their affair. He claimed extortion. She also said he was the father of her child, which proved to be false after DNA testing. Another issue? Lisa Miceli, who claimed she'd had a two-year affair with Michael. She sold the story to the *National Enquirer* and said she was going to write a book about the affair (which she never did).

9. *Tiger Woods:* Perhaps the most surprising scandal of our time, the quintessential "good boy" Tiger Woods gave new definition to the term *infidelity.* Married to stunning Elin Nordegren and a father to two beautiful children, the filthy rich, incredibly talented athlete seemed to have the perfect life and a squeaky-clean reputation to match. Little did the world know what a serial cheater this professional athlete actually was. When news broke of the first mistress (after a car wreck), the skeletons literally fell out of the closet—about a dozen of them, to be exact. Sponsors dropped him, resulting in an estimated $5–$12 billion loss. How did this cheater get caught? Tons of mistakes: text messages and voice mails acting

as the main culprits. Tiger supposedly admitted to his wife (they've since divorced) that he had over 120 affairs during the course of their marriage.

10. Henry VIII: One of the most notorious men in history, this king had six wives and numerous mistresses, including Mary Boleyn, the sister of the infamous Anne Boleyn. Anne Boleyn most notoriously refused the king's sexual advances and played hard to get, which resulted in an eventual marriage. When she was unable to birth a son, the king fostered a plan to execute her, accusing her of adultery, incest, and high treason. She was beheaded on May 19, 1536.

CHAPTER THREE

"It's Physical"

"The one charm of marriage is that it makes a life of deception absolutely necessary for both parties. I never know where my wife is, and my wife never knows what I am doing. When we meet, we tell each other the most absurd stories with the most serious faces."

—OSCAR WILDE, *THE PICTURE OF DORIAN GRAY*

CHEAT-SHEET TALE
A DAY IN THE LIFE OF A SERIAL CHEATER

I got married too young to a beautiful woman. I wish there were a law that prohibited marriage until at least the age of thirty, so the young, guileless men of this world wouldn't fall so hard and realize, so many years later, that they don't know how to be a husband.

My wife wanted kids right away. I was in love, and I wanted to make her happy, so I agreed. Becoming a father changed my life, but I guess it didn't change the part of me that craved something beyond the confines of marriage. I have always been hypersexual, and at first, my wife went above and beyond to keep me happy. But, once we started having kids, things changed. She became exhausted. I became dissatisfied. We grew distant at times. I wanted more.

Today, we have five children, a few who are becoming adults, and a couple who are just comfortably growing into childhood. In that time frame, I've had over twenty affairs. I have become a master at it, as terrible as that sounds. When news of Tiger Woods broke, I actually sighed in relief—knowing I wasn't the only one who had such an addiction to the opposite sex, this indescribable physical need to be with different women. However, my wife has never suspected anything. I guess that seems almost impossible, but she stays so busy with the kids, she has never had time to notice. Or, perhaps she is just in denial.

If people knew about my indiscretions, I'm sure they would think I'm some kind of monster. But I'm not. I still have a good heart. I help people. I volunteer. I donate. I just want what I want. I love my wife, but she has always been so obsessed with the kids. I am still healthy and attractive, still sexual, still alive. My wife and I have a healthy sex life, but it's never enough. I'm not satisfied. And isn't part of a marriage about being satisfied?

Do I think it's right? Absolutely not. It's not something good people do, and I realize I have a problem. I hope women read this and understand that if they suspect anything, look for every clue you can. Even the sneakiest cheaters can get caught.

SURVIVAL-GUIDE TOOL
CHEATER'S TOOL KIT EXPOSED

This kit is an example of items sneaky cheaters might pack with them on a daily basis (when they say they're going to the gym, to the office, or on a business trip). Search your partner's belongings for clues or out-of-the-ordinary items that he would not need on a regular basis.

- Mouthwash/mints/gum
- Tissues
- Disposable razor/shaving cream
- Condoms/spermicide
- Extra shirt/boxers/pants
- Small garbage bag (used if any stains get on clothing)
- Stick stain remover
- Cologne
- Soap
- On-the-go toothbrush
- Lint roller (used to remove any female hairs from shirt or jacket)
- Cash (withdrawn over time so partner does not get suspicious)
- Prepaid cell phone (when communication needs to be made, the disposable phones allow no calls to be traced back)

UNCOVER

SNEAKY CHEATER RULES

Not all cheaters are equally sneaky. In order to catch the sneakiest cheaters, you must first understand their thought process. Knowing how they cover their tracks will make it easier for you to catch them.

But you might ask: "If he's so good at hiding what he does, how would I even *know* to suspect him?" All cheaters, no matter how sneaky, give off clues. And one of the first clues is your own gut instinct. Women *know* when something is amiss in their relationship. Don't ignore that feeling.

Even the sneakiest cheaters make mistakes. For instance, they can become less attentive in their relationships. If he is normally affectionate and suddenly pulls away, seems distant, loses interest in sex or affection, talks less, is "tuned out" or is daydreaming, picks fights, or suddenly seems more interested in working late or staying out of the house rather than being with you, these could all be clues. He could spend more time on his phone or computer or have an increased need for privacy. He could suddenly have to run more errands or decide to take up a new hobby, even if it seems like something out of the ordinary for him. Cheaters need privacy, so they will take it however they can get it.

In some cases, infidelity makes the person more enthusiastic about his relationship, so he might flood you with affection or come home in a better mood than expected. Watch for unusual behavior shifts. Ask him a lot of questions. Sneaky cheaters usually have no problem lying, but they often don't remember where they said they were or who they were with if they are making up an excuse on the spot. Be sure to pay attention to the details and then throw a curve ball into the equation.

For example, if he tells you he was out with Joe on Tuesday night, let a few days pass. Then ask, "So, when you were out with Carl on Tuesday, did he say anything about his job? The last time I talked to him . . . ." If your partner continues this thought (not even remembering he said he was with Joe instead of Carl), then this is a definite sign of infidelity or of him hiding something. Try to trip him up with the details, as any cheater, no matter how "experienced," will make mistakes if the other partner is tuned in and aware. Other signs are as follows:

1. Sneaky cheaters pick someone they do not see on a daily basis. Though the most common affairs are work-related, sneaky cheaters refrain from cheating with coworkers. Out-of-town affairs are often the easiest to get away with. Cheaters make sure they have few personal connections with their lovers. They steer clear of friends of coworkers and friends of friends. This distance makes it easier for them to get away with cheating.

TIP. Verify his travel details by getting the hotel information and checking his credit card statements to make sure they reflect proper travel arrangements. Before he leaves, check his suitcase and toiletry kit for unusual or suspicious items (like condoms or specific grooming items he would not need on a trip away: massage lotions, different underwear, a new outfit that isn't work appropriate). Look for excessive cash and even presents he may be planning to give to the other woman. Is he excited when he returns? Does he seem "revived"? Many men who cheat while away feel completely relaxed when they return and filled with a new source of happiness. If he's supposedly "working," this sense of relaxation probably does not make sense.

If your partner does not go out of town but runs a lot of daily work errands, you can follow him so you know where he is and who he's with. If you establish his routines (for instance, if your partner goes out for lunch a lot, show up at his work and discreetly wait for him to come out), you can follow on foot or by car. If you are following by car, make sure to stay a few cars back (and only employ this tactic if he's traveling a short distance). Having a camera to snap pictures of what you see can be used when you confront him, if you don't wish to confront him at the time of the occurrence.

2. Whenever possible, cheaters keep communication verbal. If they do talk on the phone or send texts, smart cheaters have passwords on their phones and usually erase all text messages immediately.

TIP. Despite the fact that they have passwords on their phones or erase texts, they may not realize that their chat histories on their computers are automatically saved. Check e-mail chats or social media chats for any undeleted conversations. You can also "bug" your partner with a small, hidden recording device on his phone or in his car. Since legal issues can come into play when it comes to recording, be sure to check your state's laws at *www.rcfp.org.* Most of the time, a recording device can come in handy if you catch your partner, confront him, and he still denies it. By having this type of evidence, proof of the affair can be laid out and even be used in a court of law.

3. *Sneaky cheaters always pay cash.* However, if they suddenly make a ton of ATM withdrawals, they have an excuse readily available and are able to provide receipts. For instance, he could say that he is paying a personal trainer under the table, he owes someone at work for purchasing lunch or a work-related gift, he likes to bet money on his favorite sports team, or that he simply does better with cash on hand instead of always using a debit card. Not wanting to leave a paper trail can be a red flag to inappropriate activity.

TIP. Make sure you keep up with your bank balance. Are there unusual withdrawals at the same time of day or night? Is there a pattern? If he tells you he is going to the gym, but your bank balance shows he removed $60 cash, this could be a red flag. If you can get an ATM receipt from your partner, notice the address of the ATM. Is it nearby, or in an area unfamiliar to you? If it's not your usual ATM and he has no reason to be on a different side of town, you can stake out the territory to try to figure out if your partner is meeting someone at a nearby destination.

4. Sneaky cheaters give excuses they can back up. Out shopping for a shirt? They come back with a shirt. Working late? They make sure e-mails, cell phone records, and even car mileage match up to where they were. Cheaters who are hard to catch always pay attention to the details.

TIP. Details can also reveal mistakes. If he is going shopping, ask him where. If you don't believe he's really going shopping, show up in the same place. If he says he's working late, call him at the office to ensure he's there. If you share a computer and the history is always erased, this is a huge clue that he is trying to hide something. Notice his routines and patterns at home especially. Is he very particular about where he places his phone or his laptop? Does he go off into a bonus room or his office for long periods of time? Does he take "work" calls or talk to his "friends" late at night? Pay attention to what could be happening right under your nose.

5. Sneaky cheaters always pay attention to their appearance. They usually come home in the same outfit they left in. They might have condoms, wet wipes, a lint roller, an extra pair of underwear, or a garbage bag to toss garments in so tracks are covered before they return home. They make sure they do not smell differently than they normally do and that their clothes are stain free.

TIP. Do his laundry. Check for anything unusual. Check your partner's car, trunk, office, briefcase, and gym bag if you get a moment to yourself. Take a photograph of what you see and check it again after a business trip or a particularly late meeting at the office. Pay attention to the details, such as what he is wearing, and note any difference. It's hard to mask a woman's hair or her scent on his clothes. He might try wearing more cologne or even keep a spare bottle in his car to mask her scent. If this is the case, remove the bottle of cologne from the car and see if you can smell anything different on his clothing.

6. Sneaky cheaters leave everything looking just as they found it. If he cheats at home, he might even take a "before" photo to make sure the "after" looks the same.

TIP. Turn the tables on him. As mentioned in Chapter 1, if you suspect your partner of cheating in your home, take a picture before you leave and check to see if anything is out of place when *you* return. You can also set up a video camera (it would have to have an extremely long recording capability or memory capacity, unless you set a timer or a motion-activated sensor) in the bedroom. If you really want to catch him in the act, stay home from work and see if he comes home with another woman. If he works from home, pretend to go out, but hang out near the house and watch for any visitors or unusual activity. It's easy for entrepreneurs or freelancers to spend a lot of time near home and fit in "time" for another woman.

7. Sneaky cheaters never mention their lovers in conversation.

TIP. Probe. Find out if there is anyone new at work or at the gym. Plan a social outing. Be inviting and open. Figure out an open-ended way to state what you are suspecting. For example: "I thought you had mentioned something about a female friend recently. What was her name again?" Or, "Do you have any female friends I could ask to join my book club? I'm thinking of starting a book club and was wanting to get some people from outside my social circle."

8. *Sneaky cheaters work hard to stay consistent with behavior and activity.* They try not to rock the boat, so as not to be suspected.

TIP. Stay tuned in. Does your partner seem especially happy after he comes home from a trip or a long day at work? Do you have sex more or less? Is he spending more time on the computer? If you pay close attention, you might pick up on more than you think, especially in conversation. If you start talking about someone who hit on you, for instance, or that you are feeling distant lately, see how your partner reacts to this news. Notice any unusual defensive or overly nice behavioral changes. Have the two of you ever even talked about infidelity before? If you watch a movie where someone is cheating, for instance, ask him his thoughts on it. Don't come out and say, "I would kill the bastard!" Let him speak his thoughts and try to pick up on anything telling, or if he acts uncomfortable with the conversation. If he is cheating, he might actually seem guilty just when talking about a movie involving infidelity. Don't overlook his reactions.

9. *Sneaky cheaters always practice safe sex.* He won't risk catching an STD or giving his partner an STD.

TIP. Look for condoms or different forms of birth control, a change in sexual behavior, or special attention paid to hygiene, especially before work or when he's going out. If he is shaving and putting on cologne when he's supposedly going out with the boys or to the gym, he could be going somewhere else.

10. *Sneaky cheaters never park at their lover's house.* They will park several blocks away. If the sneaky cheater's lover gets in the car, the cheater makes sure the seat is returned to its proper place, the radio

station is set to the normal one, and there are no unusual scents in the car.

TIP. Though cheaters are careful, there's always the chance that they'll forget to reposition the seat or reset the radio station, so be alert to those minor variations. You can "rig" the passenger seat by putting a marker on the floor and seeing if it's still there at the end of the day. (However, if your partner typically has friends or colleagues in and out of his car, or if he's a real-estate agent, for instance—this can be harder to discern.) Search for hairs on seats as well. If you think your partner is cheating nearby, again, follow him to his destination to see what is really going on. You can also place a digital voice recorder under the passenger seat of the car before he goes out.

11. Sneaky cheaters are especially careful about how they end an affair. Rarely does it happen that two people want to end an affair at the same time. There's often a lot of emotion and anger. A smart cheater knows how to temper that emotion with explanations like, "Why would you want to be with someone who is a cheater and a liar?" or "I have to figure out what I want, and I can't do that while we are having this affair."

TIP. If your partner is ending an affair, more likely than not, he will be stressed or paranoid. Notice any unusual behavioral changes, daydreaming, or moodiness. These can clue you in to what's really going on. If you suspect you know who the other woman is, start talking about her. Tell him you were thinking about getting together with her to hang out or befriend her. Or even lie and say that the two of you are going to coffee together, or already have. Notice his reaction. Is he appalled? Angry? Anxious? If he asks, "Oh, really?

What did you two talk about?" and seems extremely nervous, this is a sign.

12. Sneaky cheaters give their partners the right to check up on them. Cheaters who are tough to catch make sure there are no loose ends. Sneaky cheaters make sure there are no photos, mementos, or evidence of any sort.

TIP. Some cheaters think that just by appearing innocent and making the offer for you to check up on them that you won't follow through. Take the cheater up on his offer. For example, politician Gary Hart challenged the media to follow him around, saying he wasn't having an extramarital affair, and they'd be bored. They followed him around—and caught him cheating. If your partner says, "Follow me around. You'll find out I'm not meeting anyone for sex," do what he suggests! If a partner gives you the green light, be the best detective you know how to be and search until you find what you are looking for.

13. Sneaky cheaters always have a good explanation if the other woman retaliates. Ending an affair can result in the dumped lover going to the cheater's spouse or partner and confessing; damaging property; slandering reputations; or punishing the cheater in any way possible. If this happens, the sneaky cheater might say, "This woman is crazy. She's accused three other employees of having an affair. She gets a crush, and then she gets obsessive and creates fantasies in her head. I swear I'm not cheating. You can check my accounts, check my e-mail, do whatever you want. There is nothing going on."

TIP. If someone contacts you claiming to be your partner's lover, listen. When people get hurt, they often have little to lose. Also, if a close friend of your partner stops coming around or your partner stops mentioning her, this is another clue that your partner may have had an affair with someone in your social circle. If all else fails, search. Search the house, the car, the office . . . anything you can to get your hands on actual evidence.

There is no such thing as the perfect affair. By utilizing technology and a little detective work, you can catch even the sneakiest of cheaters. It just takes a little patience.

CHAPTER FOUR

"It's Emotional"

"The moment you cheat for the sake of beauty,
you know you're an artist."

—DAVID HOCKNEY (ARTIST)

IT'S NOT PHYSICAL, IT'S EMOTIONAL

*I told him my secrets: how I had kissed another girl in the seventh grade,
how I had been raped by a neighbor when I was only sixteen; how I
once saw my mother strike my father with an iron and fell a little bit
out of love with the idea of romance.*

*I told him these things because he wasn't Barry. He listened to me
over coffee, when really I should have been studying French.*

*Lately, I had gotten lost in my relationship and my job. I had become
a girlfriend and a hair stylist and nothing else. I felt uninteresting and
needed a hobby. I hated sports and I wasn't an artist. At the very least,
I wanted to be able to say, "Yes, I speak French," if someone asked at a
party: "Do you speak any other languages?" So, Jason came to the rescue,
letting me fumble over words, while he gently corrected me and gave me
stacks of homework that I would e-mail back to him each week.*

At home, Barry teased me about my new endeavor. He had become sloppy and mean. He criticized my looks, my cooking, and my general talkative nature—so much so that I started to feel like I lived with my father and not a boyfriend.

I found that Jason listened to me—a small thing to many people, but it was one of the only things I cared about. One afternoon, I asked him over to dinner.

"Sure," he said.

I didn't tell him that Barry wouldn't be invited. I feared he wouldn't come. When he arrived, an expensive bottle of French wine in hand, I told him it would just be the two us. He seemed almost relieved.

As we dined, my heart leapt around in my chest. Is this what a different relationship might feel like? Real conversation over dinner? Candlelight? Filet mignon? I wanted this man, and suddenly, I didn't care about the consequences. I rose from my side of the table and crossed over to him. He leaned back, assuming I was going to clear his plate. Instead, I straddled his lap and kissed him hard. Our tongues met, right there in the middle of my dining room. This act of boldness was something I would never normally do—not even with Barry.

I knew I wanted to break up with Barry, but I was afraid of his reaction. He had a short fuse. What would he do once he found out he'd been betrayed? Hit me? Strike me with an iron as my mother had done to my father all those years ago? Did we even own an iron?

Jason and I continued our e-mails. I stored them in a safe place, memorizing each one, so lost in the idea of him. After only two weeks of meeting Jason in secret and months of tender letters, I told Barry I wanted to break up.

"Why?" he screamed.

"Because we're not friends," I said. "You never listen to me." It was a partial truth.

"Did you ever think I don't listen because you never say anything worth listening to?"

Barry made a big production of packing his bags and moving out. No one had ever dared break up with him before, and I knew he'd tell all his friends that he was the one who ended it. I continued to see Jason. I never told Barry the truth about our breakup, but I know that what I was looking for wasn't physical. It was emotional. And Jason filled that void in me, made me stop settling, and proved that I could be with someone who appreciated me for me. The path to get there was not a righteous one, but I am happy. And I hope Barry is too.

THE HEART OF EMOTIONAL AFFAIRS

Emotions are tricky. You can't touch them. Sometimes you can't explain them. They can develop instantly, without any warning. An emotional affair can start quite harmlessly at first. Two people become friends, and from there, the emotional connection blossoms.

These affairs can *sometimes* be easy to spot, as your partner will spend his time thinking about the other woman, making plans, daydreaming, and becoming emotionally and sometimes physically distant from you. He may stop confiding in you or change his habits. He might stop initiating sex and tell you that he's tired or stressed. He might start hanging out with his "friends" more or take up a new hobby, one that may involve the other woman.

Emotional affairs are difficult because they usually involve confiding and fostering a sense of closeness through intimate conversations.

Pay attention to your own emotional closeness with your partner. Are you good friends with him? There is a vast difference between loving him and liking him—these are two completely different emotional connections. To spend every single day with someone, you have to like who he is at the very core. Do you feel he regards you as a friend? What kind of conversations do you have together? Are they surface conversations, or can you discuss what is meaningful to both of you?

If he feels criticized all the time, for example, he might seek out someone who is not critical. If you don't open up to him or you turn him down for sex all the time, he might look for someone who is more emotionally and physically available. If you talk too much or complain or seem stressed all the time, he might seek out someone who is more carefree. He is searching for an outlet or a sense of newness. What he really wants is a fantasy.

Staying happy and close are keys for satisfaction in any relationship. Make sure that you are both doing your part to maintain a good emotional connection, so he doesn't look for it elsewhere. Don't be afraid to communicate and tell him exactly how you feel and what you need, and be sure and give him room to do the same. At the end of the day, knowing that you and your partner are friends and remembering the connection that sparked the attraction in the first place is a great place to start when reconnecting emotionally.

SURVIVAL-GUIDE TOOL

ALIBIS YOUR PARTNER MIGHT GIVE IF QUESTIONED

If you think your partner might be cheating or thinking of cheating, nonchalantly throw out some of these questions and see how he answers. Refer to the answer key to see how his answers stack up.

1. Where were you?
   A. I was at the gym.
   B. I stopped at Home Depot to look for some stuff for the house.
   C. I was out shopping for baby clothes.

2. You smell different. What is that?
   A. Yeah, someone was wearing really strong perfume in the elevator. I think it smells horrible.
   B. They had some new soap at the gym. I washed up with it because I forgot my deodorant.
   C. On the way home, I actually stopped off at this field of flowers and frolicked in them for a while. It was magical.

3. I kept calling you. Why didn't you answer?
   A. I left my phone in the car, and then I saw I had a million missed calls. I was freaking out. Is everything okay? What happened?
   B. I was on the other line. Sorry. What's up?
   C. Have you ever heard of this little thing called voice mail?

4. Are you sleeping with someone else?
   A. Are you?
   B. If by someone else, you mean someone who is suddenly suspicious of me for no apparent reason, then yes?
   C. Oh, yeah. I forgot to mention that I fell in love last week. We're getting married. I'll send you an invite.

5. I think you're lying to me.
   A. Well, I think you may have some trust issues. I think you always have, but that's not my fault. I haven't done anything to make you think I am lying to you.
   B. I'd rather be lying on you, frankly. Can we go do that?
   C. About what? I told you that you haven't gained weight.

6. Did somebody sleep in this bed?
   A. What do you mean? In our bed? What are you talking about?
   B. Why would you even ask that? What's going on with you lately? Is there something you're not telling me?
   C. Yes. We were attacked by midgets over the weekend, and they really insisted on sleeping in our bed.

7. Why aren't we sleeping together?
   A. I could ask you the same question. I thought it was something with you. I was trying to give you your space.
   B. Why don't you ever just attack me? Why do I always have to initiate?
   C. You're the one who seems disinterested, not me. I'm trying to be patient. My hand has been filling in for you lately, but it's really not the same.

8. I know you're lying to me. You'd better tell me what's going on, rather than me finding out. Are you cheating?
    A. Are you serious right now? How could I cheat? No one even pays attention to me. Especially you.
    B. Why don't you trust me? What have I done to make you think I'm lying?
    C. Are you projecting? Is there something you want to tell me? Are you lying? I think you're lying. There, now we're both suspicious for no reason.

9. I printed out your phone bill and there's a new number I don't know. You're calling it at all hours of the day. Who is it?
    A. It's someone I'm trying to land a potential deal with at work. Why are you going through my bill?
    B. One of my best friends from grade school found me on Facebook, and we've been talking lately. I forgot to tell you.
    C. I adopted a child in Africa, but she won't arrive for another month, so we've been talking long distance.

10. You don't seem interested in sex anymore. What's going on?
    A. I am incredibly tired and stressed. I just don't feel like it lately.
    B. I don't seem interested? You don't seem interested. Look, all couples go through lulls. Let's try to reconnect.
    C. Oh, that's because I found someone who actually *wants* to have sex with me, so I'm good. Thanks for asking, though.

Mostly A's: These answers seem genuine and not fabricated. Either this person is a good liar or he is telling the truth. Since cheaters rarely fess up, it is important to get concrete evidence before attacking or accusing them. If they ever do confess, it is often after they have already been found out. The confession is usually a last-ditch effort to keep the relationship intact.

Mostly B's: This type of person never answers the question directly. They are deflecting—perhaps out of cleverness or because they really don't have anything to hide. When this type of person cheats, he will try to turn the attention back on you. Don't let him change the subject. Make him answer the questions.

Mostly C's: These answers suggest the person does not take anything seriously, which can be a sign of infidelity. Being overly sarcastic, overly defensive, critical, or guilty are all signs someone is cheating. Sometimes the easiest way to tell if someone is cheating is just by paying attention to his behavior. All people have behavioral patterns that might shift if they are seeing someone else, falling in love, or are unhappy in a relationship. Just be aware of anything out of the ordinary.

UNCOVER

ROADMAP TO PREVENT AN EMOTIONAL AFFAIR

Since emotional affairs usually develop over time, there are many questions you can ask yourself about your relationship to see if you or your partner might be headed into emotional affair territory. Emotional affairs usually start with emotional distance, so by staying aware of your emotions and your partner's, you can better identify when something is amiss. Follow the roadmap to see where you stand with your partner, and how you might be able to enhance your own emotional connection.

West: If this doesn't sound like your relationship, the emotional distance could be caused by a plethora of things, such as stress at work. Pay attention to these triggers; if you're feeling stressed, try to be open about it and communicate with your partner. Encourage your partner to do the same. Make sure your friendship comes first so that your partner doesn't seek out that closeness elsewhere.

Good for you if you never feel emotionally distant. Even in the best relationships, this is hard to come by. When do you notice the times you are closest? Having sex, having a conversation, or all the time? While some couples prefer an independence from each other, make sure you aren't just going through the motions. Some couples who think they are actually fine sometimes ignore the most common warning signs. A dip in your sex life, close friendships with the opposite sex (or the same sex, if you are gay), constant business trips, changing computer habits, becoming more secretive, or taking more pride in physical appearances can all be signs that there might be something else going on. Pay attention to the signals and keep enjoying your healthy relationship!

Never. Head West.

West: There could be several reasons why routines change. If you've ruled out work or personal life stressors, look a little bit deeper. Are you spending less time together? Does your partner seem like he is daydreaming, withdrawing, or lacking in physical and emotional affection? Don't be afraid to tell your partner exactly what you need and what your concerns are. Open the door to communication.

Roadblock one. You may have noticed several triggers, such as a drop in intimacy, dying passion, withdrawn conversation, or your spouse spending more time on the computer. If this sounds like your relationship, head East. If not, head West.

East: Symptoms such as these can lead to emotional affairs based on confiding in a new companion. Most partners don't feel this closeness counts as an affair if it's "emotional" in nature. Watch out for friendships that could grow into a deeper attraction between your spouse and another person. Look out for phrases such as "We're just friends," or if your partner insists on being alone or becomes less intimate. A good way to combat this is to confide in your partner and make sure you foster closeness by spending time together and finding intimacy, even if it's in everyday situations. Be open emotionally so your partner feels safe confiding in you.

Yes. Head North.

Head East.

You Are Here. Start: **Do you feel emotionally distant from your spouse?**

Sometimes.

All couples feel emotionally distant sometimes. Every couple goes through lulls, and the longer you are together, the harder it can be to keep that excitement going. Focus on rituals and habits that you enjoy together, such as getting coffee, sleeping in, or watching a movie. If your partner always initiates or plans dates, take him by surprise and do something out of the ordinary. Make sure you are treating each other like friends.

If your partner suddenly starts working long hours or meets new people, don't immediately jump to the conclusion that he will cheat. Look at the circumstances and consistently remind yourself what you have to offer in the relationship. Emotional affairs often start because your partner doesn't feel comfortable sharing something with you. He may feel like he can confide in someone new, a person he may be attracted to and who won't judge him. But if he develops an emotional bond with someone outside your relationship, that can forge the path for infidelity. Make sure you are providing that sense of love and security for your partner so he doesn't feel the need to find that connection with someone else.

No. Head South.

You don't feel emotionally distant from your spouse, which is a good thing. However, do you find yourself enjoying each other's company, confiding secrets, laughing, and still engaging in sexual activity on a regular basis? If so, head East. If not, head West.

East: It sounds like you have a firm grasp on the fundamentals of your relationship. Always watch for shifts in the balance between the two of you; if your partner suddenly becomes distant or changes physical or emotional patterns, for example. Often, emotional affairs lead to sexual affairs, and an emotional connection can be even harder to break than a physical one.

CHAPTER FIVE

"It's In My DNA"

"Men are liars. We lie about lying if we have to."

—JAY LENO

BAD-BOY BEHAVIOR

I knew he was cheating. He would leave for days at a time and come up with these ridiculous stories about where he was. I was such a good girlfriend, though, and I cared for him so much that I turned a blind eye. I was only eighteen when we met, and my naiveté was in full swing. If I had been older and wiser, I would have left him.

But I was in love. I used it as my excuse for everything. My girlfriends would say: "He forgot to call you!" And I would reply: "I'm in love." My girlfriends: "He just called you a bitch!" Me: "But I'm in love." My girlfriends: "He didn't come home all night!" Me: "But I'm so in love." For me, it was enough.

One night, his best friend Joe called and invited me over. Once there, I saw Kay sitting on the couch. Though I trusted Carlos most of the time, there was one girl I'd seen him with time and time again: Kay. The way she always hugged him just a second too long made me want to slap her.

I went ahead and sat beside her. We started talking, and I felt myself relax. Somehow, we ended up talking nonstop for three solid hours. It felt good to laugh with another female. I'd been spending so much time with Carlos, I realized I had neglected my girlfriends.

As I was preparing to leave, Carlos walked in. He stopped dead in his tracks when he saw us. I looked up at him expectantly, excited to have made a new friend. As soon as he propped his bike against the door and crossed the room to sit down on the couch, I saw fear flicker across his face.

"Ladies," he said. It was almost a whisper, and Carlos never whispered. Immediately, I knew.

I looked at Kay. "Are you seeing my boyfriend?"

"I wouldn't exactly say we're seeing each other," she said.

"But you're fucking him."

She shrugged and looked at Carlos, who was avoiding eye contact. "Am I right?" I asked. "Carlos? Am I right?" I kicked his shoe.

He clenched his hands together.

"Well?" I screamed. "Answer me!"

All of a sudden, Carlos jumped up and for a horrifying moment, I thought he was going to hit me. Instead, he began waving his arms wildly in the air. "Fine, Jen. Yeah! We're fucking each other, okay? Aren't we, Kay?" He began making jerking motions with his arms and pelvis, trying to simulate sex.

I felt the rage well up. I lunged at him, but Joe grabbed me. He forced Carlos outside. My hands were shaking. I turned to Kay, suddenly exhausted. I noticed a pimple on her chin. Her hair was limp. She wasn't very pretty. This should have been comforting, but it wasn't. I still wondered what she had that I didn't. Why the love of my life had chosen her over me.

Strangely, I wasn't mad at her. I was just relieved that after months of suspecting it, I finally knew the truth. I wanted every last detail of what had happened, so I would never get back together with him. I knew he would never come clean. He was one of those people who had no conscience about lying, and he'd spin the truth to make it sound logical.

I now know to stay away from bad boys. I won't settle, and I won't fall for any guy's line. I thought what we had was true love, but I realize I was the only one doing the "loving," and it wasn't enough.

Looking back, there are so many questions I wished I'd asked Carlos when I first suspected him. They call it women's intuition for a reason— so start listening to it. Perhaps if I would have asked him questions and really listened, I would have realized what he was doing. But, I lived and I learned, and now I know what to look for.

SURVIVAL-GUIDE TOOL
BAD-BOY RED FLAGS

We've all been attracted to the bad boy. You know exactly who he is and what he looks like. He's the guy with the tattoos, the motorcycle, the cigarettes, and the bad attitude. He has beautiful eyes and strong hands and appears indifferent to the world. In your mind, he's been hurt emotionally and is secretly a romantic, so you assume he's just waiting to be saved. A bad boy is that wild, forbidden, reckless man of your dreams who makes your heart pound and ache at the same time. You swear to yourself you're not going to get involved, and yet you do anyway. Perhaps you think you'll be the one to reform him. You will be the one woman he falls for. This is usually not the case.

If you do get in a relationship with a bad boy, be prepared to have your work cut out for you. Bad boys can lie, cheat, blow you off, get defensive, or make you feel crazy. They can play mind games and say hurtful things. It's important to stay aware of where you stand with your partner. If you become suspicious that he could be cheating or his behavior suddenly changes, check for the following red flags:

1. He stops calling you. If you have had constant communication and he suddenly stops calling you, this could be a sign that he's no longer interested, he's playing a game, he wants more attention from you, or he's getting it elsewhere.

2. He's never affectionate with you in front of other women or his friends. Some people don't like public displays of affection. But, if you are normally pretty affectionate in public and he suddenly stops holding your hand or treats you like a buddy in front of his friends, or especially in front of other women, this could be a red flag that he doesn't want to appear attached.

3. He refers to you as his friend. If you know that you are his girlfriend, but in public he refers to you as his friend, he may not be able to give you the kind of commitment you want or need. If he thinks of you in his mind as just a friend, then he could be allowing himself to see other women.

4. He calls you names when you are fighting. Though tempers flare when you're fighting, watch out for particularly aggressive or harmful behavior. If he calls you names, throws things, or acts as if he is going to physically harm you, this can tell you a lot about his character. Be wary of immature, harmful behavior.

5. He never makes plans. If he never takes the initiative to make plans with you, ask him why. If you are the only one who seems interested in planning dates, this could mean several things: he's keeping you around because he knows you're available, he's using you, or he doesn't care enough to take you out. A relationship should not be one-sided.

6. Everything is on his terms. If what you do together and when you do it is always guided by his ideas and is always on his terms, this exemplifies his selfish behavior. If he never asks you what you want or need, or isn't concerned about your feelings, he may not be ready for a serious relationship.

7. You can't reach him by phone or text. If you can't ever get him by phone or text, this could mean he doesn't care to talk to you, he doesn't want you to know where he is, or he wants to maintain his privacy and he doesn't feel he needs to answer to you. Whatever the case, make sure he knows you are not comfortable with this behavior.

8. He only calls or stops by late at night after he's done partying. If he always contacts you at the end of the evening and doesn't invite you out, this could mean you are just a booty call. To him, you may only be good enough to fill his sexual desires and not much else. Usually, you aren't his only booty call. He might have a list he goes through, depending on who he feels like being with on that particular night.

If you have noticed any of these red flags, it might be time to ask him questions about your concerns. You might think, "Why would I ask him questions? He's just going to lie about everything."

The point in asking questions is to see *how* he responds. The way someone responds to a direct question can tell you a lot about what he may or may not be hiding. Since a bad boy can often have an immature response, he will give off certain body language that might indicate he is lying or hiding something. He won't look you in the eye. He gets fidgety. He gets overly aggressive or defensive. He walks out of the room. He turns everything around on you. He brushes you off. Pay attention to indicators of him not being truthful. Remember, when you ask your partner questions, try to do it in person and not over the phone so you can see how he responds. Here's a list of questions to ask and possible responses bad boys might give:

1. Is anything wrong lately? You seem unhappy.

Possible responses:
- "I've told you nothing's wrong."
- "Why are you so overbearing?"
- "I'm not unhappy. I'm fine."
- "Would you get off my back?"
- "Why does something always have to be wrong?"

Watch out for abrasive or abrupt responses that don't really answer your question. It's not unusual for bad boys to just brush off your questions. By avoiding the question, he feels he hasn't done anything wrong and he doesn't owe you any kind of explanation. When asking questions, remain calm. If he doesn't open up to you, back off. You won't be able to get it out of him by badgering him. Bad boys are the kings of the "I don't care" attitude, which is usually just covering up their past hurts and resentments. By showing that you care without coming on too strongly, you can slowly work your way in. If you back off to give him space and he still never answers your questions, this could be an indication that he is hiding something.

2. I've noticed you've been working more lately. Is there anything I can help you with so you're not so stressed?

Possible responses:
- "I'm working late because someone has to make money."
- "No, I don't need any help."
- "I'm not stressed. I'm just exhausted."
- "Sure, why don't we switch places and you can see how tough my job is. That would be helpful."
- "I don't want to talk about work right now."

While a bad boy might still brush you off even if you are showing concern, being attentive but not pushy shows that you care without being overly motherly. Often bad boys will deflect questions or try to act like they are unaffected. You must be patient when they have problems and almost mimic their air of indifference if you are try-ing to figure out what's really going on.

If he honestly seems exhausted, he might just be overworked. If you live together, see if his pay stubs reflect his extra time at work. If he simply comes home late or tells you he's working, there's no harm in swinging by his place of business to see if he's there if you are suspicious of an affair. If you don't accuse him of cheating (even if you think he is) and instead take matters into your own hands by doing a little detective work, asking him direct questions, and studying his responses, you might be able to calmly get to the bot-tom of the matter.

3. I've noticed you're spending a lot more time on the computer. Tired of me already?

Possible responses:
- "Yes. I'm tired of you."
- "Why do you think I'm tired of you every time I try to take some time for myself?"
- "I'm working."
- "A little Internet porn never hurt anyone."
- "My computer doesn't nag me."

Joking can be a roundabout way of asking if he's looking at porn, talking to someone new, or even engaging in an online affair. It also shows him that you have been paying attention to what he is doing, but aren't overly concerned. While he's not likely to come right out at that moment and say, "Yes, I'm having an affair! See?" you can still glean a little of the truth by the way he either brushes you off or tells you what's wrong. If he says, "Yeah, well, my computer doesn't nag me," that might be an indicator that he feels like you nag him too much and he just wants you to lighten up. If he continues to stay on his computer or phone more and more, you might look for an opportunity to check his phone or computer when he's not around.

4. Why do you always go in the other room to answer the phone? It makes me feel like you don't trust me.

Possible responses:
- "It's just because I don't like talking on the phone in front of other people."
- "I just want my privacy."
- "No, you don't trust *me*, obviously."
- "Whatever. You're paranoid."
- "You don't talk to other people in front of me either. What does it matter?"

Bad boys like their privacy. They can often seem paranoid and become enraged when things don't go their way or all of the attention isn't on them. Showing him that he doesn't have anything to hide can instill a secure environment that most bad boys are lacking. Again, keep your cool, address the issue, and then move on. If he turns the tables on you by saying you don't trust him, this could be a sign that he is hiding something. If the behavior continues, eavesdrop. Listen for clues, such as any unusual conversation or whispering. If he starts to whisper, walk into the room and see how he acts. Is he nervous? Does he change the subject? Does he stop talking? These are usually signs that he is talking to someone he is interested in.

5. You never compliment me anymore. It makes me feel like you're not attracted to me.

Possible responses:
- "What are you talking about?"
- "You never compliment me!"
- "Every time I give you compliments, you just say 'whatever,' so I stopped."
- "God, why is it always *something* with you? I never feel like you are attracted to me, but I don't bitch about it."
- "What am I doing wrong now?"

Bad boys usually like sex. They are physical beings. If your partner has suddenly grown distant or cold, it could be because he has found someone new. If you bring this to his attention and he brushes you off, not to worry. Start giving him compliments, or better yet, attack him in a fit of passion and see how he responds. If he tells you he's too tired or he's not in the mood, something is wrong. Men don't often turn down sexual advances, no matter how tired they are. But, don't beat around the bush with bad boys. If they are making you feel bad, speak up. Sometimes these guys walk all over their mates and don't have a sense of respect and they don't realize what they're *not* doing—like not telling you you're beautiful. It's important that you feel attractive and desired. Make him know that you are desirable and that you are comfortable in your own skin.

6. I've noticed every time we try to talk, you get defensive. One of the things I love about our relationship is that we are friends. Just talk to me.

Possible responses:
- "There's nothing to talk about."
- "I'm tired of always defending myself."
- "Whatever. I get defensive just because you are always attacking me."
- "You're the one who gets defensive, not me."
- "I don't feel like talking right now. You talk enough for the both of us."

Bad boys often don't talk about what's going on. Some men have a hard time communicating or opening up. If he doesn't want to talk, show him you can be one of the boys. Go out and have a beer. Hop on his bike. Watch the game with him. Be content to just hang out. More likely than not, if he becomes comfortable, he might be willing to open up.

If a man constantly feels attacked or criticized, however, he will be less willing to confide in you. Listen to the way he responds to this question to see if there's any truth in it. If there is, perhaps lighten up and change your approach with how you talk to him. Instead of telling him he's lazy, for instance, or he never talks, maybe you can ask him if he wants to go for a walk, or just write him a letter. A different communication approach might solve the problem.

7. What can I do to spice up our love life? I am so attracted to you, but I don't feel the attraction from you lately.

Possible responses:
- "You're crazy."
- "You can like sex for a change."
- "I'm sick of always being rejected."
- "What are you talking about? You don't even seem attracted to me."
- "I don't know. Have sex with me more than once a month?"

If you don't feel the attraction from him and he is usually very hypersexual, be concerned. If a man suddenly stops having sex, there's usually something else going on. If he brushes you off in your response, this could be a sign that he's being satisfied elsewhere.

Hunt for clues. Search his clothes for perfume or stains, and monitor his activity. Is he going out more? Are there times you can't reach him? If you make a sexual advance at him, does he brush you off? Pay attention to all the little red flags and signs that he could be cheating. If he's really not cheating and just seems uninterested in sex, be open to ideas and suggestions. Bad boys will often challenge you in the bedroom. They like sex and adventure. This goes both ways. If you want him to do something he's not doing, speak up.

Asserting yourself and showing him that you are sexy and adventurous will keep both of you satisfied.

8. You seem really distant and I never see you anymore. Why are you pulling away?

Possible responses:
- "I'm just busy."
- "I'm not pulling away."
- "Why do you always have to be concerned about something?"
- "I just don't have enough time right now to hang out with you."
- "I just need to spend some time alone for awhile."

If he's pulling away from you but not from anyone else, or he still makes times for things he enjoys but just not for you, then he could be losing interest in the relationship. He may feel smothered, bored, or just need some time alone. Show him you're in the relationship for the right reasons and that you care about him, but that you will also give him his space. And ask yourself if you *are* suffocating him. Do you have interests outside your relationship? You don't always have to be so available to him. Sometimes bad boys like the "chase" and for their partner to still have some edge of mystery. If he says he needs time "alone," this could be true, or it could be because he is interested in playing the field. Give him space, but keep your eyes open for any unusual activity.

9. Every time we're out, you're hitting on other girls. How would you feel if the situation was reversed?

Possible responses:
- "Why are you always so jealous?"
- "You think I hit on everyone."
- "Whatever! Flirt with whoever you want. I don't care."
- "I have a lot of girlfriends. But that doesn't mean I want to sleep with them."
- "I don't care who you flirt with."

Bad boys are flirts, and they don't see anything wrong with that. But, there's a difference between flirting and being disrespectful to you. If he's obviously crossed the line but says he doesn't think there's anything wrong with his behavior, this should be a clue to how he could be acting when you're not around. The next time you're out, flip the switch. Don't be overly flirtatious, but be friendly and open. Don't pay a lot of attention to him, and show him that you are attractive and if he wants to be with you, he needs to pay attention. Let him know his behavior is one-sided and unfair.

To recap, when asking questions (not only of a bad boy but of any male in general), pay attention to uncomfortable body language, and watch out for the following behaviors:

- He becomes overly defensive.
- He switches blame by redirecting the conversation back to you and then refocuses on something you've done.
- He accuses you of not trusting him.

- He calls you crazy or paranoid.
- He ignores you and brushes you off.
- He calls you possessive or tells you that you are smothering him because you are questioning his every move.

If your gut instinct tells you something doesn't feel right and your partner is exhibiting any one or more of the above behaviors when you question him, it could mean it's time to put on your detective hat to find out the truth, or simply end the relationship.

HOW LIKELY IS HE TO CHEAT?

1. Your partner is online late at night and an ex pops up on instant messenger. The conversation turns flirty. The ex asks what your partner is wearing. Does he:
   A. Tell her he's wearing nothing
   B. Change the subject
   C. Log off quickly
   D. Go tell you what just happened

2. You're out with your friends and your partner gets hit on. It's late, he's drunk, and the person asks for his number. Does he:
   A. Give her his number
   B. Ask her for her number and then gives her a fake number
   C. Tell her he's in a relationship
   D. Tell her that his girlfriend wouldn't like that, and if she doesn't leave him alone, you will kick her ass

3. You are experiencing major problems in your relationship.
   He's been hanging out with a friend he's attracted to at work.
   You ask him if there is anything going on. Does he:
   A. Get defensive and start yelling that you are crazy and jealous
   B. Laugh it off and tell you nothing is going on
   C. Apologize and ask how he can make things better
   D. Tell you that he enjoys spending time with his friend
      because she just seems to understand him more

4. You see that your husband's ex is calling. You are having rela-
   tionship problems, and his ex asks how it's going. Does he:
   A. Tell her how tough it's been and that he isn't happy
   B. Change the subject
   C. Tell her that he's never been happier
   D. Try to make his ex jealous by regaling her with stories of
      your current relationship

5. How many times has he cheated in previous relationships?
   A. A few times
   B. Who? Him? Cheat?
   C. Never
   D. Only once, but he told you all about it

6. You find out that your partner cheated on you. Do you:
   A. Immediately retaliate
   B. Act like you don't know
   C. Talk it out and decide if you want to leave or stay
   D. Retaliate, make him beg for forgiveness, and then spend
      the next year of your relationship punishing him

7. What kind of relationship did his parents have?
   A. They got divorced during his teenage years
   B. Divorced before he could talk
   C. Still together
   D. His mom/dad had more boyfriends/girlfriends than you can possibly keep count of

8. What's the most important part of your relationship?
   A. Sex
   B. Laughter
   C. Love
   D. Desire

9. What is most important to you?
   A. Knowing your partner desires you
   B. Knowing that you are friends
   C. Knowing that your partner is faithful
   D. Knowing that your partner finds you absolutely irresistible and would do anything for you

10. When you are out together and there is an attractive woman in the room, does he:
    A. Ogle her in front of you
    B. Make a comment when he notices you noticing her and tells you that he's allowed to look
    C. Doesn't even notice her
    D. Berate you for being jealous and tells you that maybe if he got laid once in a while, he wouldn't be looking

Mostly A's: Cheater in the Making

He seems to play with fire and is flirtatious by nature. Though this type of behavior may seem harmless, talking to past lovers and focusing on physical attention can often lead to affairs when things get rough in a relationship. He needs to remember why he is with you and try to give you as much attention as you require. It's not all about him.

Mostly B's: Oblivious Flirt

He seems to brush off flirtatious advances and makes light of everything. He might find himself in compromising situations if he isn't careful, as he seems oblivious to how his behavior might come off to you. Be careful of his past lovers and make sure he stays respectful of your relationship's parameters. If people come on to him, tell him he can say no and doesn't have to be so flirtatious. He doesn't have to be so likable all the time.

Mostly C's: Faithful to the End

He is open, honest, aware, and faithful. He knows why he's in a relationship, and he isn't afraid to speak his mind or tell you when he is unhappy. He knows how to be a listener as well. Keep up the great work, and enjoy a faithful union!

Mostly D's: Button Pusher

He likes to push buttons and make you jealous. He likes attention, but that attention doesn't count unless you recognize that he is desired. This need for attention could be covering up deep insecurities and lead him down a path of cheating. Don't expect your partner to give you attention all the time, and don't give him attention all the time. It takes two people to make a successful relationship and making someone worry all the time isn't fair. Be honest with him about your feelings and what you need to be happy, and then *listen* as he tells you the same.

CHAPTER SIX

"People Lack Discipline"

"If you marry a man who cheats on his wife, you'll be married to a man who cheats on his wife."

—ANN LANDERS

CHEAT-SHEET TALE
BECOME YOUR OWN PRIVATE PI

It was late one night, and my husband was supposed to be gone on a business trip. He'd become more distant lately, and I had a feeling that something was going on. I called his cell phone and he answered, telling me he was on the way to a business dinner.

"What hotel are you staying at again?" I asked. After I hung up, I called the hotel and asked for my husband's room. He wasn't even checked in there. I don't think I've ever felt so sick. I remember holding the receiver in my hand and a feeling of dread spreading through my entire body. I was being betrayed by the man who told me he loved me and would forsake all others.

I was horrified at becoming another statistic. I loved my life. I loved my husband. Sure, our relationship wasn't perfect, but there was no one on earth I'd rather have pizza and a beer with. We laughed. We still had sex. We talked. None of this made sense to me.

Scared but on a mission, I decided to take matters into my own hands. When he returned, I welcomed him with open arms, and then told him I actually needed to go out of town for a few days for a business trip, which wasn't unusual in my line of work.

The next morning, he made me coffee and dropped me off at the airport. Once there, I rented a car and checked into a hotel a few miles away. It was a weekend, and my husband said he was just going to lie low with a few drinks and a movie. That night, I got into my rental car and drove down our street, parking a few houses away. I watched our house like a hawk, vacillating between feeling like an idiot and a scorned woman.

Much to my horror, around 8:00 P.M., I saw a beautiful redhead walk down the street. She didn't look nervous or out of place. She walked up to my house and knocked. My husband opened the door, and she disappeared inside. Suddenly, my entire world shifted upside down. Not only was he cheating on me, but he was cheating in our home. *The home that we'd bought together. Our sacred space we hardly ever even had friends over to, because it was such a haven. Part of me wanted to scream. Part of me wanted to go back to not knowing. And part of me wanted to take a fucking baseball bat to his skull.*

I opened the car door and stood in the street like an idiot. I walked to our front door and turned the knob, knowing that after this moment, my life would never be the same. They were in the kitchen, her skirt hitched up around her thighs. She couldn't have been more than thirty years old. My husband's hands were all over her. Hands that had held my hands on our wedding day, hands that had touched my body for eleven years, hands that had wiped away my tears, hands that had cupped my swollen stomach as I suffered through two miscarriages. Terrible one-liners built up in my head, and I couldn't think of anything clever to say.

So, instead I blurted, "She better be wearing underwear." It was the only thing I could think of—this woman's bare ass on my clean countertops.

"Kate." Richard looked at me and dropped his hands from his mistress. I took a step forward. "Why?" I asked. "Just tell me why men do this? Why do you have to do this? Why can't you be satisfied with just one vagina? Do they really feel that fucking different?"

Before he could respond, I glared at the woman. "Get out of my house." And because I felt that wasn't harsh enough, I added, "whore."

"Richard?" She ignored me completely and looked at my husband. The intimacy with which she said his name revealed this wasn't a short-term affair. That's what gutted me the most. She said his name the way I'd said his name a thousand times: there were secrets in the way she said his name. Memories. Promises, even.

A week later, I filed for divorce. In that week, I went through every emotion one can possibly go through. I thought of murder, suicide, forgiveness, guilt, failure, popping pills, becoming a nun. . . . I honestly didn't know how our relationship had become susceptible to an affair.

Once he moved out, I realized how many clues I'd missed. He was smart about his affair, but there were still clues: unfamiliar e-mails, greeting cards from another woman, clothing I had never seen, different cologne, and condoms (which we didn't use). Items I hadn't even paid attention to. The number one clue I missed? His business trips. He was having an affair on these so-called trips, and I had no idea. He would even pretend to go out of town some days, and instead stay with his lover. I didn't know how relatively easy that would be to pull off until I booked a fake trip and checked into a hotel myself.

Because of my husband, I don't trust men. I thought Richard was one of the good ones . . . and now I don't even know what that term means. What constitutes a good guy, and how do you ever really know?

If he really wasn't happy, I wish he would have simply told me. Sometimes I feel like people would rather be stuck in a loveless relationship than venture out on their own and dare to be alone. As soon as things get "boring" at home or you get stuck in a routine, you immediately start fantasizing about being single again or meeting someone new. I thought our relationship was immune to that stuff. But guess what? No one is immune. It can happen to anyone, anywhere.

HOW TO BECOME YOUR OWN PRIVATE INVESTIGATOR

Private investigator and author Guy White sees the behavior described in this story all the time. He refers to it as the cloak-and-dagger syndrome: "People are bored," he says. "They actually cheat out of boredom, to make their lives more like James Bond. An affair becomes that excitement they don't get from their jobs. But it's not always sexual. Some of it is just getting away with something. People like the rush and excitement of sneaking around. It gets old eventually, and that's when they get caught. Where they fall short is when they have children. Then it gets really messy."

Guy had a female client who told him that her marriage wasn't going so well and that her husband traveled a lot. Guy asked where he traveled to, and she said he went all over the country.

"How do you know he does?" he asked. "Do you call him at the hotel, or do you call his cell phone?"

"His cell," she replied.

"He could be on his cell a block away, and you wouldn't know."

This is just one example of how cheaters can deceive you. So, how do you act as your own private detective if you are suspicious of a cheating partner? According to Guy, you can do many things:

1. Look for unaccounted-for time. Unaccounted-for time means time when your partner is away from you, supposedly doing other things. He might have set routines or hobbies, which you never question him about. For instance, does he go to the gym twice per day, or for extremely long periods of time, but his body doesn't show improvement? Does he work more than normal, take long lunches, or not take or return your calls for long periods of time? It's important to look for areas of time where he may say he's doing one thing but could be with someone else.

INVESTIGATING UNACCOUNTED-FOR TIME

If you suspect your partner of cheating, one of the first things you can do is find out what he's doing with his spare time.

The Gym Excuse

If he goes to the gym more than normal (and he is not an athlete or extremely diligent about fitness), check his clothes when he returns. Are they sweaty? Do they smell like he was at the gym? To take it a step further, ask him specifics about what he does while there: what kind of routines he follows, what kind of cardio, classes, and strength training. Ask him for specific exercises that you could do and see if he can show you any. Or, better yet, if you are not a member of his gym, tell him you are going to join so you can get healthy together. Notice his reaction. Does he try to discourage you from going to the same gym?

Does he seem nervous? What does his body language say? Study his response.

The "I've-Got-to-Work" Excuse

Does he suddenly work later than normal or take more business trips? Don't just assume he's up for a big promotion or has to stay late because he tells you he does. It's easy to tell you one thing and then do another. If you have access to his credit card statements or his paycheck, see if either reflects his overtime or traveling expenses. If he's working late, ask him questions about his work. Does he give you details about what he does or just sum it up quickly? Is he resistant to talk about what he does when he's not with you? Express interest and see how he replies. If he tells you about how his boss has been riding him, that's one thing. If he says, "You wouldn't understand," he could be hiding guilty behavior.

If he is working later, call the office or simply show up to bring him a late dinner. If he's traveling, ask him if you could tag along (if you can clear your schedule). Explain that you would just enjoy a few days away at a hotel. If he doesn't have anything to hide, this shouldn't be a problem. Again, notice his reaction and body language when you talk to him directly about these things. If he says, "Oh, you'd be bored," or "It's not really a place to relax," or, "I don't really think we can afford it," he might be hiding something.

The Out-to-Lunch Excuse

Does he take long lunches? And how would you know if he *does* take long lunches? Try calling him on his lunch break, or call his work to find out where he is and with whom. If you can't get this information easily, make plans to meet for lunch and see if he is happy to oblige or says he is too busy to meet. You are looking for pockets of time when he is supposedly busy. Many men use this time to cheat, since it's the only time they can fit it in. If he says he is going out to lunch (and this becomes a pattern), check for receipts or ask him specifics about his meal or about the restaurant in question. For instance, if your partner supposedly goes to the same restaurant all the time, show up. If he's not there, call him and ask him where he is. If he tells you he's there, then you know he's lying and can set the stage to discover where he is and with whom.

The "I'm Away from the Phone, but Please Leave a Message" Excuse

Are there specific periods of time when you can't get him on the phone, but he still has a proper alibi? Do you try to call him or text him and later he says, "I was in a meeting," or "My phone was on silent. Sorry," or, "I never answer my phone when I'm at the gym." If it happens once, that's understandable. If you try to call him during the same time every single day and you can't get him, you might want to take a closer look at what he could be doing.

2. Install a GPS in a car or on a cell phone (see the "Cheating Gadget Guide" in Chapter 6 for specifics). This is truly one of the most effective tools to figuring out where he's going and what he's doing. Instead of stealing his phone when he's not around or following him around like a stalker, you can track his activity remotely with a small stealth device.

3. Check cell phone records, and also search for a second, secret cell phone. Many people receive their cell phone bills online or set up an automatic payment plan. To obtain cell phone records, you normally need the owner's social security number, last name, cell phone number, and his password. If you know this information, you can set up an online account through his carrier. If he already has it set up this way but you don't know his password, you may be able to reset his password so you can log on. Password change alerts are generally sent to his e-mail address, however, so you would need to be able to check his e-mail if you are going to reset a password. If he gets paper statements, go through his mail when he's not looking, or check in a filing cabinet to see if he stores bills there.

Once you have the cell phone records, you can look in detail at who he is talking to and write down any unfamiliar numbers.

Some men also carry an extra cell phone. Look for places such as the glove compartment, a briefcase, a nightstand, a drawer near an entrance table, his office, or even the trunk of a car. Check his pockets or jacket pockets as well. If there is a period of time when he's taking a shower or you are alone near his regular cell phone, scroll through it to see who he's been talking to. Text messages and photographs are two areas to check immediately. If he has a password set on his cell phone, and he has a phone with a SIM card, remove his SIM card and see if it will plug into yours so you can immediately access his information to see what he is doing or possibly hiding from you.

4. If you ever follow your partner on a regular basis, employ the front-tail tactic. Instead of a traditional tail that involves following someone in a car from a safe distance, you actually drive in front of the car you are following. This works best if the person is suspicious of being followed. Get in front of the car and pay close attention to where he is by using your rearview mirror. He will never suspect being followed. This tactic, often used by private investigators, takes a bit of practice to master, which is why GPS is often most effective.

5. If you follow your partner to a place where he is cheating, take pictures or video of the vehicle in proximity to where it is for proof. If you want to wait until your partner comes out, see if you can catch him in the act and snap photographs to avoid an ugly confrontation. If you don't need proof, confront your partner directly and let him know that he has been caught. Since these situations can sometimes escalate, many individuals prefer to get the evidence first and deal with a confrontation later.

Either way, it is important for you to acknowledge the truth of the situation so you can figure out how best to deal with it.

6. Look for hidden decoys. A hidden decoy could be used to throw you off the scent of a cheating partner. For instance, your partner might start talking excessively about someone he isn't remotely interested in, just to steer your attention in a different direction, while he secretly cheats with someone else. Cheaters are clever and often think you won't go to the trouble to check into their stories or alibis.

If you have a gut feeling about someone in his life, ask him about it and watch the way he responds. Does he seem edgy or nervous? Defensive? Also listen for elaborate excuses if he's late, has missed an appointment, or flakes on plans. If he tells some incredibly detailed story that doesn't make a lot of sense, chances are he's lying. He could use a friend as a decoy, involving him/her in the story so he can do something else with another woman.

As another hidden decoy, he could also purchase a set of golf clubs, a guitar, or other arts or sports equipment to make it look like he is getting serious about a new hobby. Test him. Have him teach you how to swing a golf club, play a scale on an instrument, or offer to go watch him practice. Does he act nervous? Does he insist you wouldn't like it or that he's not ready to have an audience? Really listen to what your partner is telling you. Pay attention to the details. This is how cheaters get caught.

7. *Make sure to build a case before confrontation.* Taking your time to gather evidence is important in any case, and proving infidelity is no different. If you just think your partner is cheating and confront him, he could get defensive, extremely angry, or deny the entire thing. Even if you know you are right, you still won't be able to prove it and will probably end up feeling crazy.

When you have photos, video, text messages, e-mails, or other evidence and *then* you confront him, there's no way for the truth to be denied. It makes the lies disappear and causes him to confront the truth head on. You might ask why you even need evidence? If you aren't married, just hit the road. If you are married or have children and are going to use infidelity as grounds for divorce, it is important to obtain concrete facts for divorce court.

According to Guy, cheating happens because people lack discipline. "Discipline is left out of people's lives when it comes to relationships. Love *is* discipline. That means you go to happy hour but come home early," he says. "That means you don't put yourself in compromising situations. It means you go home and see your wife or husband. That's the discipline of relationships. Sometimes people just need attention and they can't control their urges. That's called weakness. People say, 'It wasn't working out between us.' Yeah, it was working out, but you just lacked discipline."

Guy points out that it's easier to cheat if you have money, because cheating requires money. If you suspect cheating, follow the money trail. Look at credit card statements, his computer's browser history for websites where he could have made purchases, and any e-mails with receipts. Cheaters will likely spend money on the following:

1. Porn (i.e., photos, magazines, videos, hard copy, or online videos)
2. Video sex chat
3. Phone sex chat
4. Lovers or potential lovers, with the hopes of getting sex; this could include travel, restaurants, gifts, sexual aids (sex toys, condoms, lubrication, Viagra), or other hygienic products that seem out of the ordinary

In order to figure out how (and if) your partner is spending cash on these items, make sure you get a handle on bank statements or any bank accounts your partner might have. See the following section, "Survival-Guide Tool: Show Me the Money," for more on this.

SURVIVAL-GUIDE TOOL
SHOW ME THE MONEY

If you have a hunch that your partner could be spending money on sex, porn, or on an affair partner, observe his financial patterns— *pattern* being the operative word. Cheaters can be careless, and this carelessness crosses over into money. Often, if you just observe the money trail, you can figure out if something is amiss.

- Obtain your partner's credit report (this is possible if you are married) to see if your partner has racked up debt elsewhere, such as with an unfamiliar credit card. A credit check will give you all accounts, their history, and debts owed.
- See how much cash he carries in his wallet before he goes to work. When he gets home, search for receipts and see how much is spent. If it seems like an exorbitant amount, keep track of it for a week or two and then confront him about his spending.
- Check e-mail for online reservations to restaurants, shows, or hotels, and any receipts for travel that you are not a part of.
- Look for items, like gifts, that are obviously not meant for you (something that wouldn't fit you or is the complete opposite of something you would like).
- Search for new porn videos, magazines, or unusual items that you have no knowledge of being purchased. Search medicine cabinets, briefcases, and gym bags for unusual products, condoms, and sex toys.
- Scrutinize sudden changes in food preferences, hobbies, or music preferences that result in new purchases that seem out of the ordinary for your partner.
- Verify that assets (stocks, bonds, etc.) haven't been liquidated without your knowledge.
- Track his spending when you're together. A sudden decrease in casual spending when you are together means he may be saving the money for someone else.

- Examine financial documents. They may reveal that he has been paying someone else's bills. If he has opened a new bank account or credit card (especially without your knowledge), it may be to facilitate cheating.

- Ask about raises, bonuses, or overtime pay if your partner isn't forthcoming about them. He may be hiding the money from you to spend on his cheating.

SURVIVAL-GUIDE TOOL

THE STEP-BY-STEP GUIDE TO BECOMING YOUR OWN PI

- Tell your partner you are leaving for the weekend and then stake out a place close to your home. Crash with a friend or family member or check into a hotel. Rent a car or borrow a friend's, and park several houses down to observe any unusual activity and track new visitors. This can be time-consuming, so be prepared to do a lot of waiting. If your partner leaves the house, be ready to follow him to see if you can catch him in the act. Remember that you are supposed to be invisible, so maintain your distance so as not to get caught.

- Place a voice-activated digital tape recorder in a discreet, hidden place such as under the bed or car seat to record all conversations. Make sure it has a large memory so it can record for many hours.

- Place a Track Stick GPS tracking device in your partner's car. You can install it near the dashboard or steering wheel or even on the outside of the car. They cost around $250, but they are no larger than a pack of gum and will track anywhere an automobile goes. Type "Track Stick GPS" in Google to find the best deals.

- Install a GPS tracking device on his cell phone. An easy way to do this is to purchase him a new phone and have it installed before you ever give it to him. Most iPhones already have a built-in GPS system.

- See what social media sites he's on, or peruse dating sites to see if he has a profile online. If so, set up a fake profile and contact him to see if he takes the bait. If he's on Facebook, set up a fake profile and "friend" him, flirting shamelessly to see if he falls for it. If you are worried about someone particular in his life, set up a fake e-mail account, pretending to be that person. Tell him you got a new e-mail address and you wanted him to have it. See if he writes back to you and what he says. Online behavior can reveal a lot about your partner's character and integrity.

- Press the redial button on the phone or dial *69. This is an effective way to find out who your partner has been calling. Also listen to new or saved voice mails on his cell phone or work phone if you have access.

- Be aware of any close platonic relationships. Most friends will not approve of the cheater's ways but will cover for them. Some friends will actually help the cheater by providing an alibi. If it's not a believable alibi, start questioning the friend. Most friends will cover for cheaters if they aren't directly involved. Once you call the friend out on a lie, he might say something like, "You'll have to ask him about that," or, "I don't want to be involved," which pretty much tells you something is going on.

- If you suspect your partner, act naturally. Although it is difficult, you must still treat the cheater the same way you did prior to suspecting him of cheating. If your partner knows you're suspicious, he will simply try to cover his tracks better or back off of the affair. Give the cheater plenty of room to make a mistake that will confirm your suspicions.
- If you have exhausted all other means of catching your partner—such as looking into financial records, checking clues around the home, the computer or his phone, and you have come up empty-handed, it's possible that he's not being unfaithful.

However, if you still feel certain he is cheating but you can't prove it, you can bluff that you "know" information. You could tell your partner you know he's been cheating and you are giving him an opportunity to fess up, and if not, it's going to be ten times worse. Remain calm, but maintain that you have proof. Tell him you had him followed. Most cheaters will lie or deny the truth, but some will come clean. If he doesn't come clean and you still feel like he's lying, it might be time to break up and move on.

Following Phone Trails

Look for unexplained, repetitive charges on cell phone bills. Often these calls will be made right after leaving home in the morning and right before coming home in the evening. A cell phone bill is one of the best ways to catch cheaters, because the bill lists every single call made (unlike a bill for conventional phone services, which lists only long-distance charges). If you suspect your partner is cheating, and he doesn't have a cell phone, buy him one and install a GPS tracker on it before you give it to him. Other phone clues to look for:

- Phone bills that contain calls with long duration
- Phone calls are not returned in a timely fashion
- An unusual number of hang-ups or wrong-number calls are received
- Partner leaves home or goes to other rooms to talk on the telephone
- Partner hangs up suddenly when you walk in the room
- Suspicious voice mails from women that are vague or cryptic, or from companies or services you are unfamiliar with
- Blocked calls to the house
- Partner receives calls late at night

Tracking Computer Clues

In addition to paying attention to your partner's phone habits and phone records, you can often catch him cheating by paying attention to how he uses his computer.

- Most people who are having affairs wipe out the information from their hard drive with programs like Window Washer, which makes them more difficult to catch, but not impossible. Key logger software programs can catch anyone. If your partner is computer savvy, and you don't feel secure installing a key logger software program, consider an external attachment, which you can find at *www.keyghost.com* for about $90. With an external attachment, you can simply clip it to his keyboard when he's not there, retrieve the information from the computer, and remove the device. You can even use it on other computers you might be suspicious of. No installation is necessary.

- Some cheating signs to watch for include using the computer alone and secretly with a demand for privacy (thus, you should be concerned if the computer is moved from a visible area to a locked office). If someone begins cheating, whether online or in real life, he'll often go to great lengths to hide the truth from his partner. Try to keep your computer in a public area at home where you can monitor your partner's Internet activity.

- Check the Internet web browser history list for unusual sites. This is an easy way to catch a cheater unless he clears his cache (memory) often or uses software to clean it. Turn off the "clear history" setting on the computer.

- They make frequent visits to free Internet e-mail accounts to cover their tracks (i.e., Hotmail, MSN, Yahoo!, Gmail, etc.).

- There are suspicious or deleted e-mail messages that seem personal in nature, romantic, sexual, from a dating or porn site, or may be unsigned and from an unfamiliar sender.

- Watch for signs of your partner being preoccupied with online chatting, or if he becomes more emotionally distant or is spending an excessive amount of time in online chatrooms.

- Note if there is excessive Internet usage, especially late at night. Chatrooms and meeting places for cybersex don't heat up until late at night, so cheaters tend to stay up later. Often, the partner suddenly begins coming to bed in the early morning hours or may get out of bed earlier for a prework e-mail exchange with a new romantic partner.

- If you interrupt your partner when he's online, watch for angry or defensive reactions.

- Watch to see if your partner quickly closes programs when you enter the room.
- Note if your partner has a loss of interest in sex. Some cyberaffairs evolve into phone sex or an actual rendezvous, but cybersex alone often includes mutual masturbation from the confines of each person's computer room. When a cheater suddenly shows less interest in sex, it may be an indicator that he has found another sexual outlet. If sexual relations continue in the relationship at all, the cheating partner may be less enthusiastic, energetic, and responsive to you and your lovemaking.

Finding Financial Clues

Although cheaters often pay in cash to hide their tracks, you may discover financial clues among your credit card bills and other receipts and records.

- His credit card bills contain unusual gifts, travel, restaurant, and unknown charges.
- You find florist or jewelry bills or receipts for cosmetics or perfumes, but they are not gifts for you.
- Income tax returns reveal unexplained travel and business expense deductions.
- You find unexplained payments on bank statements.
- Your partner has more cash on hand without accountability.
- Your partner has unexplained receipts in his wallet, glove compartment, or office desk.
- You discover the recent opening of another checking account.
- There's an increase in ATM withdrawals. Check the transaction record to determine the withdrawal location, time, and date. If

the location is somewhere completely out of area, keep track of who he might be meeting nearby.

- There are unexplained withdrawals from your checking account.
- The time and date of an ATM withdrawal is recorded at a time when the spouse should be elsewhere, such as at work.
- Gas credit cards contain atypical locations of gas stations.

Checking for Car Clues

Cheating almost always requires a change in driving patterns so that the cheater and his lover can get together. Here are some things to look for:

- A change in your partner's driving pattern. You may find the car needs gas more often or you may monitor the car's odometer and find your partner is putting a lot of unexplained miles on the car. Monitor your partner for two weeks. During this time keep track of the mileage on his car. Monitor the time he leaves for work and the time he comes home. By keeping a calendar and noting the times, you may discover a pattern. If your mate claims to be working late, check paycheck stubs to verify this overtime.
- Credit card gas purchases are inconsistent for the amount of miles driven on the car.
- Your partner explains a late return home as a result of having to drive out of town on business, but the mileage on the car indicates fewer than ten miles driven.

Identifying Behavioral Clues

Your partner's behavior will almost always change if he's having an affair. He may become more distant, judgmental, or blame you for his behavior. At the beginning of an affair, he may actually be more affectionate than usual due to guilty feelings. After the affair has been going on for a while, he may start finding fault with you as a defense mechanism (i.e., to justify the affair in his mind). Other signs he may be thinking of (and sleeping with!) someone besides you:

- Joins a gym or weight reduction clinic
- Begins visiting tanning salons
- Gets a new hairstyle
- Wears cologne more often
- Starts excessively buying new or different clothing
- Gets laundry done independently
- Engages in more frequent bathing and more careful grooming
- Exhibits to you an unexplained indifference or aloofness in the relationship
- Makes spontaneous plans or events that do not include you
- Is often distracted and daydreaming
- Asks about your schedule more often than usual
- Increases his Viagra usage
- Pays less attention to you
- Shuns things like shared baths, talking over the dishes after dinner, or renting a video on a Saturday night
- Doesn't get as excited about taking vacations together and avoids talking about long-range relationship plans
- Spends unaccounted time away from home
- Exhibits a change in sexuality (i.e., more sex, less sex) as well as unexplained sexual requests
- Says he's "too tired" when you feel like being romantic
- Comes home late

- Becomes defensive during normal conversations
- Ignores household chores
- Loses interest in domestic activities, such as spending time with the kids, fixing up the house, lawn care, etc.
- Starts bringing you flowers and acts especially nice or doesn't bring you flowers anymore and acts especially mean
- Brings up someone else in conversation all the time
- Tells you he just hired a new assistant and that she is not very attractive, but, when you meet her, she is absolutely gorgeous (if your partner isn't cheating, or thinking about it, he shouldn't lie to you about this person's appearance)

Changing Work Habits

Your partner's work habits—or claimed work habits—will probably change if he's being unfaithful. For example, you should be suspicious if he:

- Comes home later than usual
- Starts working late or hanging around with buddies after work
- Is often unavailable at work
- Attends more work functions alone
- Suddenly has abnormal work hours

CHEAT-SHEET TIP

If your partner starts demonstrating any of these behaviors, do a little research. Try to stay calm, even if you are suspicious. Gather evidence, then confront your partner. Don't think he will fess up when confronted? See below for the "Cheating Gadget Guide," which provides and explains tracking software for catching a cheater.

CHEATING-GADGET GUIDE

These clever gadgets and computer programs can help you discover if your partner is cheating on you:

- *Tracking software.* One example: PC Pandora Key Tracking Software/PC Pandora: PC Surveillance and Internet Monitoring (*www.pcpandora.com*). PC Pandora is your very own personal PC and Internet detective that hides on your hard drive and monitors all computer and Internet activity. This program will allow you to record and take snapshots of the websites visited, e-mails sent and received, instant messages sent and received, chatroom conversations, and other computer and Internet activity on your PC. This software can also be used as a key logger that will allow you to record secret passwords that someone may want to keep hidden from you. Once you know the passwords, you will be able to enter any site that someone tries to keep hidden from you, or log in to secret Gmail, Hotmail, Yahoo!, AOL, or other web-based e-mail accounts.

- *Online asset searches.* One of the best sites out there, Tracer Services (*www.tracerservices.com*) performs asset searches, background checks, cheating-spouse searches, phone searches, postal searches, and more. It checks cell records, as well as collect calls and third-party billed calls. Want to know exactly where your partner and his cellular telephone is? If his cell phone is turned on, you can use the cellular phone network to pinpoint the exact location of his cellular phone anywhere in the United States. You give a cell number and you will be provided with the current GPS coordinates of the telephone. The phone must be turned on and in the United States.

- **GPS tracking devices.** These devices help locate a vehicle at all times. One can be found at *www.rmtracking.com*. It can tell you where the vehicle is in actual time, where it was, and where it is going.

- **Cell phone searches.** For those who are more interested in what's going on with phone calls, *www.clubmz.com* is for you. For a very low price, you can listen to live calls, extract text messages, look at photos, and read call logs, all in one software package. If you visit the website, you can download it immediately. There is no paper trail through the mail, and it is the same system law enforcement uses. A similar service is available through *www.cellspyarsenal.com* and *www.e-stealth.com*. You can monitor iPhone usage in real time with software from *www.mobile-spy.com*. You install a software application on your phone. The program starts every time the phone is turned on, but the user won't know that. The information gleaned by the software is uploaded to a special account on the Internet. When the phone is on, its GPS location is recorded every half-hour.

- **Spy cams.** If you want a discreet way to record activities, visit *www.spycameras.com*. Using all-in-one cameras, body-worn cameras, nanny cameras, or night vision cameras, you can easily plant an unseen camera in the suspected cheater's office or on his personal property.

- **DNA testing.** Check out real DNA testing kits at *www.infidelity today.com*. An infidelity test kit will quickly and easily monitor your partner's sexual activity outside of the relationship by detecting traces of semen left in his undergarments after sex.

THE CHEAT-SHEET TIP

Before using any of the spy tactics mentioned in this book, please check your local and state laws so you don't break the law. If you do break the law and your cheating partner discovers how you caught him, he could use it against you in court.

CHAPTER SEVEN

"Workplace Affairs"

"I guess the only way to stop divorce is to stop marriage."

—WILL ROGERS

CHEAT-SHEET TALE

CONFESSIONS OF A PERSONAL TRAINER

I wasn't happy with my marriage, even though we'd been together for nine years. The passion was gone. My husband and I never communicated. Everything was always my way, and he went along with it. Because I got my way, we never fought. And if there was a fight brewing, he would just back down and drop it. Our relationship went on like this for years.

Despite that, we were extremely social and always had a good time. We made good money, and I decided to pursue a big dream of mine and become a personal trainer. I quit my comfortable corporate job and started working at an elite gym.

Gyms are the worst, in terms of infidelity, because of all the people and the nice bodies. If you are having problems in your marriage, it is a dangerous place to go. Physiques are exposed and dripping with sweat . . . endorphins are kicking in. You are accomplishing physical feats, and you are usually in a good mood. Basically, it's one big sexual playground.

When I got hired, I noticed one of the trainers, Greg. He was attractive. Because we worked together, we saw each other every day. I saw Greg more than my husband. The flirtation started to build. It had been forever since I'd felt anything in my marriage, and I wanted—no, I needed to feel something. I got enamored with the idea of being naughty. I was so responsible, so respectable, and I was tired of being the good girl.

When the affair started, I felt guilty. After the very first time we slept together, I began to cry. "No, this didn't happen," I whispered. "I didn't just do that. Please, no. No. No." I pretended it didn't happen; I prayed that it hadn't, because I knew that my life from that moment forward would be divided into two parts: before and after. I now had a secret from my husband, one that I couldn't take back, and one that would forever change that day and all the days to follow.

But I let my wild emotions and the indescribable passion take over. I felt attractive again, I felt ravaged, I felt hungry. So this is what it feels like, I thought. This is what it's supposed to be. I was exhilarated. I was feeling things again.

Suddenly, my world was reduced to only two things: guilt and longing. Greg and I were completely reckless. Everyone at work knew I was married. We found out years later that all of our coworkers knew. Everyone knew we were having an affair. Even gym members. We were the talk of the gym. But, in our eyes, we were in our own little world.

My husband didn't suspect anything. I wasn't acting any differently at home. My love for my husband became my comfort. He was my safety blanket. He was making the money—I know that sounds horrible— but I was financially secure. I was secure with our home and with having a husband. I liked my role as his wife.

One weekend, my husband went out of town, and Greg and I had a romantic weekend set up. He came to my house, but I couldn't do it.

We didn't even step foot into the bedroom. We slept on the couch. It was too weird. He was in my husband's territory.

Once he was in my home, the reality came crashing down. So, finally I said, "I can't do this. I want my marriage to work." I immediately quit the gym and found another job.

Though things didn't go completely back to normal, my husband and I floated along for a few years, until he came home from a trip and said, "I want a divorce. I'm tired of trying to make you happy. I can't make you happy, and I want to be happy. So, I'm done."

I was utterly shocked. In my mind, I thought just by making the decision to be in my marriage should have been enough for it to work. That's the whole ironic thing. Though he never found out about my affair, my husband left me anyway.

SURVIVAL-GUIDE TOOL
PREVENT WORKPLACE AFFAIRS

Work can be an intimate environment and can provide the temptation to stray. After all, your partner is with his coworkers more than he's with you. He may develop commonalities and friendships with them. He may be attracted to a coworker, and the close proximity of the workplace can allow the attraction to grow. Almost 90 percent of all affairs begin at work.

Clues to look for:

1. If your partner talks about a coworker a lot, pay attention. Ask specific questions about the coworker and see what your partner reveals. You could ask: "So, what does her husband/boyfriend think about that?" Gently find ways to probe about her lifestyle, to see how much he knows, or how much they talk about personal details. If he says, "Oh, she's having problems in her relationship," or, "Her husband's a jerk," this proves that they have discussed their relationships, which can lead to dangerous territory if it's not strictly a platonic friendship.

While it's great for your partner to have close friends, if it seems like there is an attraction, stay aware. Listen to the details he reveals, or if he just happens to mention her in random conversation. It's natural when you are first interested in someone to start injecting that person's name into casual conversation. This is a common clue of a budding attraction.

2. If your partner interacts with a coworker in a flirtatious manner, be concerned. Rarely is flirtation just harmless. It usually leads to something else, even if it appears innocent. Watch the way they interact together. Does she touch him a lot, stare at him longer than normal? Does she pay attention to you, or ignore you completely? How does he act around women in general? If he is willingly flirting in front of you, this could be cause for concern as to how he could be acting when you're not around. Pay attention to these clues. If you question him about it and he brushes you off, remind him that his coworker might be getting the wrong message. Mixed messages can be sent all the time, and sometimes men are not aware of their behavior.

3. If your partner mentions that he has asked a female coworker for advice about your relationship, tell him that he needs to set boundaries. If he airs your problems in front of someone he's attracted to, it hurts your relationship and creates a common bond between them. While he might not see it that way, ask him how he would feel if the situation were reversed. Men like attention; they like feeling like problem-solvers or asking for advice from time to time. Remind him that an attractive female coworker is not his primary audience, and if he wants advice, he needs to talk to you—his partner.

4. Play a game with your partner. Ask him what he would do if you gave him permission to do whatever he wanted with a coworker, without consequences. Consider his reaction—if he laughs out loud, that's one thing. If he seems intrigued, that's another. If he does seem intrigued, probe further. Even offer to go first and set the stage to be open and honest. See if he takes the bait to discuss what he might do with someone else. By playing out these scenarios you may discern what he feels is lacking in the relationship, or what he's looking for. If he admits that he would have a one-night stand, he could be looking for that spark or passion. If he talks about taking a trip or wants to wine and dine someone, maybe he's looking to be romantic.

5. Find out a bit about his coworkers. The more you know about them and can talk with him about them, the more likely you'll spot if something in his relationship with one of them changes. For instance, if you make it a habit to discuss what happens during his workday and how everyone is doing, and he stops talking about one coworker completely, take notice. While sometimes men talk more about someone they are interested in, they can also stop talking about that person completely, or talk derogatorily about them to throw you off the scent. Watch for sudden changes.

6. If he tells you that someone in the office keeps hitting on him, be concerned. He may be enjoying the attention. A man not interested in straying would nip an advance in the bud. If he mentions it once or twice, it's probably nothing. Flirtation can be natural (and sometimes men think women are flirting when they are just being nice). He could even try to make you jealous if he feels unwanted or undesirable. If it becomes a daily habit of him "complaining" about someone's advances, tell him how you feel. If he is enjoying the attention, it might be a good time to look at your own relationship. Do you give him attention? Do you get attention? Does he feel wanted and attractive? Is there anything that can be tweaked to make both of you feel better? Communication is key.

7. Keep your own work relationships strictly platonic and aboveboard. That way, if he starts throwing your concerns back on you, you know he's being defensive and possibly hiding something. If he knows that you keep your professional relationships strictly platonic and that you are only interested in him, he cannot turn the tables on you as a diversion.

8. In order to keep his thoughts on you while at work, write your partner a love letter and e-mail it to him. Or send him a sweet text. Let him know you are thinking of him. Sometimes a gentle reminder of his real love life can take him out of a potential fantasy with someone else.

UNCOVER
HAPPY AT HOME

You come home at the end of the day, and you are exhausted. Your partner is exhausted. You have your routine: unwind, have dinner, and sit in front of the television, where mindless reality TV takes over for the next few hours. You get sleepy and then go to bed. If this becomes your day-to-day routine, how do you keep yourself satisfied at home? When do you make time for sex or quality conversation, when all you feel like doing is nothing?

First of all, don't let anything get boring. Don't take each other for granted. Routines aren't necessarily bad, as long as they are enjoyable. If you make dinner all the time, go out. If you go out all the time, make dinner. Find time to connect. Talk to each other. So often, men or women talk all day in their jobs, so when they come home, they just want to unwind. Be willing to give your partner that time if he needs it to relax, take a shower, exercise, or whatever he desires, for a specific amount of time. Don't get defensive if your partner needs alone time away from you. Be respectful of his boundaries and find a way to make your time together enjoyable. Sometimes it isn't about the quantity of time, but the quality of time.

Focus on what used to make you happy. Some couples think they can't be as spontaneous as they were in the beginning once they have mortgages, kids, and full-time jobs. Yet, the greatest moments are often the smallest moments. Taking a walk after dinner, getting into a massive laughing attack, turning your bed into a fort, eating dessert by candlelight in the bathtub, cuddling in bed, holding hands while sitting on the couch, reading each other poetry, playing a game, giving each other a massage . . . all of this can help you bond. Get creative. Be loving and attentive and try to make your home space sacred.

It is often hard to let your job go at the end of the day. In America, most people are so obsessed with working, making ends meet, and acquiring more, more, more that they often lose sight of what is the most important thing: relationships.

On average, Americans spend eight hours per day at their jobs, and they are so committed to them that they neglect their relationships or look for a quick fix when they get tired of their current situation.

Try to let go of all of your massive to-do lists at the end of the day, or at least designate a time to work on them so that you can spend more quality time with the one (or ones) you love.

One of the easiest ways to reconnect is by having sex, but so often women, especially, are too tired. You must make sex a priority. It is often why people stray in the first place. If you know you are going to be tired at the end of the day, attack your partner right when he walks through the door. Or meet for lunch for a "quickie." Make time for foreplay. Touch your partner when you are cooking or when you are talking. Focus on the details that turn you on. It doesn't have to be a long, drawn-out session. Duck into a closet. Use the countertops. Bring some excitement to simple situations.

Sex is one of the most enjoyable aspects of *any* relationship. Learning to reconnect and coming home to something exciting and fulfilling should be part of everyone's daily routine. Make it a priority every day for a week and see what happens.

Remember: long-term relationships take constant care and reassessment. Perhaps you are completely content with the way things are, but your partner might be missing something and is just too afraid to speak up. Relationships are as much about the other person as they are about you. It takes two people to be happy, and you have to find that happiness in yourself first before you can find happiness with another person. Don't be afraid to communicate, and try not to get defensive if your partner says something you don't like or agree with. Oftentimes, couples build up a million tiny resentments. Try to drop those resentments and really listen to your partner, or ask him to listen to you.

Remember that you can make your relationship whatever you want it to be. There are no written rules that say because you've been together a certain amount of time your relationship has to be sexless, joyless, or boring. You can revitalize your union at any time. You just have to be willing—both of you.

CHAPTER EIGHT

"Online Affairs"

"I change my mind so much I need two boyfriends and a girlfriend."

—PINK

A CYBERWORLD

We'd been dating for five years. We'd even discussed marriage, but if you are a gay woman, you still don't necessarily get the same rights as everybody else.

Right before our anniversary, Tracy and I started fighting. She brought up stupid things and started pulling away. We weren't communicating. We stopped having sex. As a former cheater, I know the signs when someone is being unfaithful, and I felt like she was hiding something. I begged her to be honest with me, but she wouldn't. So, I looked for the obvious clues. Did she smell different, were there any stains on her clothing, hidden receipts or text messages? Normally, she left her phone out. For two weeks, she kept it with her at all times, even when she went to the bathroom. When I asked her why, she said her boss had been riding her.

"Since when?" I asked.

"Since always," she snapped. "Why are you being so suspicious? Are you projecting?"

I was impressed with her ability to try and take the focus off of herself and put it onto me. She seemed nervous and on edge. I knew Tracy. If there was anything to be found, it would be on her e-mail. One day while she was at work, I sat down at our computer and logged on. There, in her trash, were messages from some guy named Travis. Could the love of my life be sleeping with a guy?

Instead of raunchy e-mails, they were sincere confessions of how he felt about her, what he thought about her intelligence, her beauty, and her radiance. These were the same things I'd told her, just in a much more eloquent way.

I didn't know which hurt the most: the fact that this guy had been writing to my girlfriend, or the fact that she couldn't bring herself to delete them from her trash. I found the e-mails she sent to him in a different file name on her desktop. Suddenly, it didn't even matter if she'd slept with him or not. It was her emotional connection . . . her emotions were all over the page.

I logged on to Facebook and searched to see if she was online. She was. Was she chatting with him right now? The irony would be too much. I asked her what she was doing. "Just working," she wrote. "You?" In another window, I logged out and logged into her account. Immediately, like in some movie, her instant messenger popped up, one with her chat to me and one with someone named Tdupont: "I want to take you into my mouth right now. I want to feel you."

"Oh my fucking God," I whispered. "Are you serious? Are you fucking serious right now?"

My hands trembled as I went back to the other screen and typed in more words. "So, who else are you chatting with? You're leaving me hanging."

"What are you talking about? Just you. Work is just slammed right now."

I read her boldfaced lie. How many times had she done this—written such innocent sentences, when really, she was getting off online with some guy?

"Okay, well I'll see you tonight," I typed with trembling fingers.

"Okay, sweetie. Love you."

When she walked through the door at her normal time, she smiled.

"Hey, baby." She dropped her purse by the door. Every morning, I tripped on it going to work and I always asked her to move it. We were going on six months of this same conversation. Suddenly, that little gesture—or her inability to do such a tiny thing that I'd asked—pushed me over the edge. She could cyberfuck some guy, but she couldn't move her purse so I could get in and out of our home? That said it all. I marched across the room, bent down, snatched her bag, and threw it as hard as I could across the room. Her lipstick and phone went flying. Her compact smashed against the hardwood floor in a powdery pile. Our dog whimpered.

"Are you fucking insane?" Tracy screamed. "What is wrong with you? My phone is in there!"

"What's wrong with me?" I fumed. "What's wrong with me?" I walked to the counter and threw the e-mails at her. "How about what's fucking wrong with you? I'm not the one cheating during my lunch break. Five years, Tracy. Five years of my life, and this is how you thank me?"

Tracy didn't move. "How could you go through my stuff?"

"Are you shitting me right now?" I shrieked. "That's what you're concerned with? That I went through your stuff? Do you know who you're talking to? I used to play this game. I know when someone is cheating."

"I'm not cheating," she said. "We've just been writing. That's all. I swear."

"Writing? Writing that you're so wet and you want to take that guy in your mouth? That's fucking cheating, Tracy, and you know it."

"But we haven't done anything!" She was growing hysterical. "You and I have just been distant, you're depressed, and you always tell me what I do wrong. It just . . . it just felt nice to get some attention for a change."

"Are you in love with him?"

She hesitated.

"Get out of my house," I said.

Sometimes people assume because I am a lesbian that the rules of monogamy don't apply. Well, for me, monogamy is monogamy. Period. And in my mind, an online affair is the same as a real affair. It usually always leads to something physical, and later I found out it did in Tracy's case. I blame a lot of it on us, but technology just makes infidelity too easy.

SURVIVAL-GUIDE TOOL

WEBSITES CHEATERS FREQUENT

In today's society, one of the easiest things to do is flirt online. Anything you want, it's out there: people are not shy about making their desires public. Even for those who don't physically cheat, the Internet makes it easy to dip in a toe and test the waters.

Anyone can meet other people online in an endless number of places. These places can be classified into the following categories:

- Chatrooms (MSN and Yahoo! are the most used, as well as Skype for video chat)

- Friend networks (*www.hi5.com*, *www.facebook.com*, and *www.orkut.com* are popular)
- Direct contact through chat profiles (Looking through the profiles of MSN members)
- Sites to match couples (*www.perfectmatch.com*, *www.match.com*, *www.eHarmony.com*, and *www.plentyoffish.com*)
- Relationship sites that emphasize sexual encounters (*www.passion.com*, and *www.adultfriendfinder.com*)

Cheater websites have become commonplace. Websites such as *www.ashleymadison.com* and *www.meet2cheat.com* specialize in promoting discreet affairs between married and committed people. Through alibinetwork.com, cheaters can be set up with virtual phone numbers, virtual e-mail accounts, and untraceable phone numbers. The service also helps them cover up lies. Some of their services even have someone come pick up the cheater at his home in a truck with fishing gear for a guys' getaway, when in actuality, the cheater is simply using this as an excuse to spend a weekend with his mistress.

Married and committed people who utilize cheater websites want to have their cake and eat it too. Unfortunately, this is usually unbeknownst to the unsuspecting partner. Sites like these tap into a very profitable market within the online personals arena by bringing honesty to the dishonest practice of cheating. They allow people an alternative to a traditional personals site where they may have to lie and say they are single, thus giving potential mates the wrong impression—but they still make light of lying to a spouse or partner.

Married people seem to seek other married people to give themselves a sense of added security in an inherently insecure position.

Their preference to cheat within their own camp is based on assumptions about people with spouses. They will not demand too much of the other person's time; they will be less invested in the relationship since they already have one; and they are more understanding about a last-minute cancellation because the wife or husband is sick or the kids need to go to soccer practice.

If you think your partner might be cheating, check out these websites, gather clues, and search his Internet history. Remember to gather evidence *before* making accusations, and figure out how you *really* feel about it before you confront your partner. Are you angry? Relieved? Do you feel crushed? Vengeful? Sorting through your emotions and coming to a rational frame of mind is of the utmost importance when deciding to break up or engage in a confrontation. If the partner feels attacked, he will often place blame, lash out, or even pretend to be the victim. Being tactical about your confrontation is key.

UNCOVER

ONLINE AFFAIRS REVEALED

In this day and age, it's pretty simple to get away with an online affair. Your partner could pretend to be doing work in another room when he's actually chatting or writing e-mails to his lover. Writing releases inhibitions for many people, because it's easy to get carried away when it's not reality. Many men don't feel it's an actual affair if sex isn't involved. However, infidelity is infidelity—even if it's happening over a computer screen. So, if you suspect your partner of having an online affair, the following red flags can help you discover the truth.

Some signs to watch for:

1. He uses the computer alone and secretly with a demand for privacy. When someone begins cheating, whether online or in real life, he'll often go to great lengths to hide the truth from you. If he's always in another room using his laptop, try to steer him away from computer time. If he feels paranoid at home, he could do most of the e-mailing or chatting at work (in which case, a key logger would come in handy).

2. Internet web browser history list (this is a record of websites visited) contains unusual sites. This is an easy way to catch a cheater unless they clear their cache (memory) often or use software to clean it. Again, many men will do their e-mailing/chatting at work if they feel they can't get privacy at home.

3. Check the computer and the trash folder for uncommon e-mail messages or suspicious, racy deleted e-mails that are sexual in nature.

4. He seems preoccupied with online chatting, is more distant emotionally, or is spending an excessive amount of time in online chatrooms or on the computer.

5. He engages in excessive Internet usage, especially late at night.

6. If interrupted when online, he gets angry. When a partner is doing something wrong and he feels he is getting caught, it is natural for him to lash out. Notice any strange behavioral changes.

7. He quickly closes programs when you enter the room and appears nervous.

8. His sleep patterns change. Chatrooms are popular at night, so the cheater could be staying up much later than normal, or waiting until you go to sleep to chat privately.

9. He loses interest in sex or intimacy. If you initiate and he pulls away, this could be an indicator that he is being satisfied elsewhere, whether online or real life.

10. He turns the volume off (or changes his settings) on the computer so the instant messaging sounds don't give away the chatting taking place.

11. Look for frequent usage of Skype or video chat programs, which may be used for free sex video chats between the cheater and his affair partner. Check accounts online to see if video chat is being used.

12. If you share a computer, check for hidden files, website history, external hard drives, or any file name that looks unusual. Look at his social media e-mails as well.

13. If your partner is on Facebook a lot, notice who he's talking to, who his friends are, etc. Is there flirtatious behavior going on? A woman who always comments on his photos, or someone he seems especially friendly with? Sometimes these innocent comments can lead to e-mails and then inappropriate behavior.

14. Make sure he's not on any cheater websites and that he hasn't set up a profile anywhere. Go to popular dating or cheater websites and do a search for his name to make sure he doesn't pop up.

15. Look for unusual phone activity, such as your partner taking the phone to the bathroom, perhaps in order to text or e-mail privately. If you are out, accidentally forget to bring your phone and say, "Can I use your phone really quick? I need to make a phone call for work." If he seems nervous, this could be an indicator he doesn't want you going through his phone.

If you suspect your partner is engaged in an online affair, stay calm. Never accuse your partner of cheating unless you have concrete proof, because the majority of cheaters will lie. Your accusations will simply prompt him to cover his tracks better next time. Most cheaters lie to protect their online affairs, which often trigger bigger and bolder lies, including denial or telling you they will quit whatever it is they are doing. Sometimes men will try to justify online affairs by saying it's not real, it's just a fantasy, or they are just bored and wanted someone new to talk to. Ask him how he would feel if you were engaging in the same behavior, and let him know that to you, it is cheating, and it will not be tolerated.

If your partner confesses to an affair and you decide to stay with him, realize it's normal to be paranoid about his computer time. If he has nothing to hide, ask if you can check up on him, or if you are still suspicious, install a key logger to track his activity online. You have to decide what your limits are. And remember, the Internet is rife with opportunities to stray.

It's very important to talk to your partner about his views on cybersex, online pornography, and the legitimacy of online adultery. Pay close attention to what he says. Does he feel that infidelity only counts if it is physical? Does he think viewing online pornography or videos constitutes infidelity? What about live sex video or chatting? Find out what your partner's definition of infidelity is so you are both on the same page.

CHAPTER NINE
"Worst-Case Scenarios"

"I married a liar. Why? Because I married a man."

—BONNIE HUNT (*ONLY YOU*)

THE AGE OF STDS

I was pretty content in my marriage. Sure, we had our ups and downs, but what couple doesn't? It was February, and I went for my annual checkup at the gynecologist. I'd been going for ten years, and I had always checked out clean. So, when I got a call one week later telling me I had cervical dysplasia, I was shocked.

"Have you had intercourse with anyone else?" the doctor asked.

I was offended. "Of course not," I snapped. "I'm married."

She cleared her throat. "And your husband?"

"We are faithful," I said.

I called my husband at work to tell him, and he was eerily calm. He wasn't overly supportive. At first, I thought it was because he didn't understand how serious this was.

Then I started to think about his nature. He was incredibly flirtatious, but that's just who he was. Yes, he had a porn addiction, but what guy didn't? And his increased business trips, hidden magazines, enhanced privacy about his text messages and computer time was normal, wasn't it? I broke out into a cold sweat on the way home. Had he cheated? Could he have actually had sex with someone else without me knowing? Weren't women just intuitively supposed to know?

After my doctor's visit, I had two glasses of wine and waited for my husband to come home. I resisted the urge to go through his things, to prove that he'd been unfaithful. I figured I would at least give him the chance to defend himself.

"Hey," he said when he walked through the door. He noticed the wineglass in my hand. "Rough day?" he asked.

I set the glass down and smiled sweetly. "I'm just going to ask you this once," I said. "And I want you to trust me enough to be honest. I need you to be honest with me, for both of our sakes. Okay? Have you been unfaithful in our marriage? Just a simple yes or no will suffice."

He looked as though I had actually slapped him. "What kind of bullshit question is that? No, I have not been unfaithful. I haven't kissed another woman since the day I met you."

"What about fucking? Have you fucked another woman since the day we met?"

"You're drunk," he said.

"No, I am perplexed, Jonathan. I'm perplexed that after nine years of marriage and three years of dating, that suddenly I have some form of an STD. Explain that to me. Explain how I am suddenly diseased. I would love to know."

"I don't know. Maybe you have something to tell me?"

"Fuck you," I spat. "You're an asshole. You don't even care that I'm going through this! You never care—just as long as you're getting laid and can look at your stupid fucking magazines and dirty pictures."

"You know why I do that? Because they aren't frigid. They actually make me feel sexual, unlike you."

I wanted to slap him. Instead I took the wineglass and launched it at his head.

"You've lost it," he said and stormed upstairs.

But I knew one thing. I knew my husband had cheated. I ransacked every e-mail, every desk drawer, every account he had. I found secrets. Pictures of ex-girlfriends, all naked, in various poses, next to ones he'd taken of me. Old e-mails and journals, hidden bank accounts, hidden debts. Everywhere I turned, there was a new secret. I told him what I'd found. He was furious, saying I had invaded his privacy and he could never trust me again.

Our relationship went downhill instantaneously. I became despondent. Depressed. I just wanted him to tell me the truth, but he wouldn't. I think he enjoyed the torture. Though that's not why we divorced, it was the beginning of the end. I lost my ability to trust him, and I lost a little of my ability to trust myself too. And once the trust went, everything followed. Now I make sure I am with someone I can trust, and who fully trusts me.

SURVIVAL-GUIDE TOOL
WORST-CASE SCENARIOS

It's a fact that worst-case scenarios occur when someone cheats. What happens if he gets his lover pregnant? Or gives you an STD? If you lose everything all because of his indiscretions? Following are some of the most common worst-case scenarios, as well as several options for dealing with them.

1. He gets someone pregnant.

First of all, you have to decide if you are going to leave him or stay. The initial reaction is to leave, feel devastated, swear off men forever, and sail off into the sunset. Reality is rife with tougher emotions, feelings of betrayal, heartbreak, and insane jealousy. If you decide to leave, try to make a clean break. If you stay, this is where the tricky part comes in. You have several options:

A. Suggest an abortion.

B. Suggest adoption.

C. Help pay for the baby but don't be a part of its life.

D. Get a DNA test to prove that he was the one who got her pregnant.

2. He gives you an STD.

You'll need to decide what to do about the unfaithfulness, but your priority should be to take care of your health.

A. If it's curable, take antibiotics or prescribed medicine.

B. If it's herpes, there is no cure. Preventative medicine helps control outbreaks.

C. If it's HPV, there is no cure, but make sure you get regular pap smears to detect any irregular cervical cells that can lead to cervical cancer.

D. If it's HIV, begin and stay on treatment.

Note: If you have an STD, you must tell future partners before you have sex with them.

3. *He sleeps with your friend.*

This is an enormous betrayal of trust, not just on your partner's part but on your friend's part. You have several choices:

A. Talk to the person he slept with to find out both sides of the story. Record the conversation.

B. Eliminate the person from your life with no further communication.

C. Refuse to talk to both of them and attempt to move on with your life.

D. Get them both in the same room and have a serious heart-to-heart so you can make an informed decision about why this happened and what you should do.

4. *The person he's with threatens your life.*

Your partner's lover may see you as a rival to be eliminated. You may be in danger even after he calls off the affair if his lover isn't ready for the affair to end. Your best course of action is to first do a bit of research about this person. Has she committed any previous crimes? Is she emotionally unstable, or just angry that she cannot have what you have? Decide what is best for you in this scenario and make sure your safety comes first.

A. File a restraining order.

B. Have someone stay with you until the situation passes.

C. Take steps to protect yourself such as installing an alarm system, buying mace, adopting a guard dog, hiring a security guard, and learning self-defense techniques.

D. Insist that your partner handle the situation immediately by threatening legal action.

5. *You catch him in the act.*

Whether you were suspicious of an affair or you just found yourself as a witness to the naked truth about his affair, you have choices:

A. **Remain calm.** There is nothing scarier than an eerily calm woman. Demand he tell you the truth—how long it's been going on and what happened. Do not let the lover get away without confronting both of them. It is important to hear both sides of the story to try to comprehend what happened, so that you don't have any questions unanswered. This can be an important step in the healing process.

B. **While your immediate reaction might be to get violent, don't.** If you can, take pictures with a cell phone, record your conversation (iPhones have handy internal recording devices), and attempt to stay calm. Get as much information from him as you can to be used in court (if applicable) or to your benefit if and when the time comes.

C. **Walk away and have no further communication.** As tough as this will be, a caught spouse will most likely grovel and beg to get back together and insist he has reformed. This is typically just remorse talking. Time usually reveals the same habits. And since cheating is usually indicative of something lacking in the relationship, unless issues are solved, the urge will still be there.

D. **If all else fails, freak out.** Go completely crazy to insure that he will never do this again and that you are *serious* about this (just don't inflict any physical harm on anyone else and realize this should be a last resort; acting out usually does more harm than good). Traumatize him so much that the next time he goes to have sex, he won't be able to.

UNCOVER
QUICK-FIX GUIDE

Though there's no quick fix to a worst-case scenario, you can do several things when faced with any of the worst-case scenarios:

- *Stay calm.* This sounds obvious, but it is vital. When enraged, emotional, or upset, you can make claims that are untrue and inflict permanent damage on your relationship. For instance, if you are dying to know the truth about a cheating partner, and you start screaming and making threats and demanding that he tell you everything, this will just make him distant and defensive. The calmer and more rational you appear, the more information you will receive.

- *Every problem has a solution.* Think of it not in a "poor, pitiful me" way, but like this: "I have a problem. What is the easiest and most creative way to solve this problem?" You cannot go through life without bad things happening. So, if you are unhappy with something, fix it. Don't dwell or obsess upon it. Become resourceful and come up with valid solutions to your problems. For example, if you discover your partner has been unfaithful, get out of town. Take a few days to figure out how you really feel and what this indiscretion means. Start making lists of all of the things you need to do if you do break up and what legalities (if any) will be involved. It's much easier to think with a clear, unbiased head. If your partner is begging you to forgive him and bombarding you with calls and texts, it's impossible to make an unemotional decision. Stick to the facts and approach this like a problem-solver.

- *Do what you want to do, not what your friends or family tell you.* This sounds simple, but you are influenced by others' opinions all day long: on television, in magazines, at work, at home, and in everyday life. Everyone has an opinion, but only you know what you can and can't live with. If your partner gets someone pregnant, can you live with it? Can you separate your own personal relationship from the fact that there will be another human being with part of your lover's DNA? If you know you can't, move on. If you can, make every effort to get past it. Approach each and every situation with your needs and wants in clear focus.

- *Know your rights.* If he gets someone pregnant, cheats, uses your money for his lover, what are your legal rights? What if you have children? Look into your state's laws and your own personal rights as a spouse or parent. There are legal aide services that are free if you don't have a lawyer. Do your research.

- *Don't make empty threats.* It's easy when you are angry to spurt out things like, "You will never see your children again." This turns the guilty party angry, so the focus is now off of them and on what you are taking *away* from them. Keep the focus on the issue at hand and nothing else. Don't use your children as ammunition when you are angry, no matter what. Refrain from taking the kids away just to be vindictive. Make rational, informed decisions. It's easy to personalize bad situations when they happen, because they are happening *to you*, after all. But, just because you want his head on a platter doesn't mean he's not a good father. Try to be as adult as possible when making tough decisions that affect not only you but your children as well.

- *Communicate.* You can't ever really know what happens in any situation unless you talk about it. Sit down and have an actual conversation. Don't just assume you know everything because you found a racy text or e-mail. Sometimes situations are not as they seem. Allow your partner to explain himself. Listen to what he has to say. *Everyone* can make a mistake. It's important to understand why. While it's not acceptable to cheat, there are usually reasons relating back to the both of you. Listen, learn, and decide what you want to do from there. Can your relationship be fixed? Do you want it to be fixed? If so, know that it will take time, work, and effort. But sometimes, the hardest decisions can be the best and most fulfilling.

- *Don't obsess.* The most natural thing in the world (for women especially) is to obsess and analyze. What does the other woman look like, feel like, smell like? What does she have that you don't have? What's he really doing at work? Is he where he says he is? Can you really trust him? Why did he look at your best friend that way? Is there something that he's hiding? This is not only a waste of time; it's often irrelevant. The reason people cheat is because they want to feel special or new. They want excitement. They want to be reminded that they are valued. Sometimes genuine love in relationships has nothing to do with someone else's actions when he is not with you. It's important to understand why people cheat and the road it often takes to get there (so you can try to prevent this from happening). However, if you and your partner split up due to an affair, move on. Do not compare every future relationship to your last one, and don't reduce your relationship to that one occurrence. It's not only unhealthy, but it can also keep you stagnant and prevent you from moving on in a healthy, productive way.

CHAPTER TEN

"Picking Up the Pieces"

"Why did God create men? Because vibrators can't mow the lawn."

—MADONNA

MY WIFE'S AFFAIR

When I met my wife, I had just graduated from college and was working at a new startup company that required frequent travel. Deedee was in graduate school and student teaching.

One night after a week on the road, I was unable to reach her. I tried again the next day but had no luck. Finally at the airport on the way home I reached her, and she said she had been working late grading papers and probably fell asleep and didn't hear me call.

It wasn't until several months later, when we were planning our wedding, that Deedee sat me down and told me what really happened that night when I was out of town. She confessed to a kiss or two with another graduate student.

I pressed her with more questions until finally she admitted that he had come over to our apartment and they had slept in our bed. She started to cry and said that it didn't mean anything. I blew up and screamed, "What do you mean it didn't mean anything!" I was so angry and hurt that I punched a hole through the drywall and stormed out. I didn't see her for days. I felt trapped because we had already announced the wedding to everyone.

She convinced me to go through with the wedding, promising that it would never happen again.

A few months later, my parents came to town and wanted to take us out to dinner and a movie. Deedee did not return home from her 4:00 P.M. class as scheduled. I called her office but she did not answer. It was almost 2:00 A.M. before she came home, her skirt disheveled, her heels in her hand. She said that her teacher had needed her help. "I had to take him all the way to Dallas to his apartment because he commutes out to the university," she said.

I told her I didn't believe her and that it was over. I stormed out of the house and sat crying at a nearby park. About an hour later, I felt her arms around me. Deedee said she was sorry and that there really was no reason for us to break up. She knew it was a mistake and that she shouldn't have let it happen. She insisted that they had done nothing more than kiss. She begged me for forgiveness.

We moved past the events of that night, mostly due to her convincing pleas and my willingness to forgive and believe her. She promised to cut all ties to the professor.

One day, years later, while searching for something else, I found a three-by-five card with a series of addresses and phone numbers on it, each line crossed out and replaced with a new one. I soon realized that it was a record of all the professor's addresses and phone numbers.

Deedee had secretly kept in contact with him for years. That night I confronted her and demanded that she tell me the entire truth this time. She was not willing to give up that truth without a fight. I had to ask question after question. She explained she had been in touch with him a few times over the years. She said that she had not resolved her feelings for him when we were married and that she had to talk it out with him. I reminded her that when she decided to marry me, that all other relationships were suddenly very final and not up for debate anymore. She insisted they did not have sex. She held tight to this claim, like it preserved what was left of her innocence. But that claim too later unraveled.

The biggest problem now was that it was not so easy to break up. We had two children whom I adored and loved.

One night Deedee's lifelong girlfriend called. I decided to take a gamble that she had confided in her friend. I told her I had found out everything and asked her what I should do. She unwittingly filled in the missing gaps and confirmed my worst fears. Deedee's affair with the professor had continued for years.

In the past, I was willing to forgive and forget, over and over again. However, the cheating and infidelity were like a cancer in our relationship. It killed not only my faith in her, but it killed Deedee's ability to be truly open, intimate, and loving with me. She withdrew more and more each year. I could not bear the pain of it all. I had an affair out of revenge. I thought that if I could equalize the situation, I would not feel so victimized and I would be less humiliated. But it only added to the distance between us. And when I told her about the affair, she was just as hurt as I was, and it only served to make things worse.

Finally, we had to explain to our children that although Mom and Dad loved each other very much, we could not live together anymore. Their pain continues, although as they grow, they heal and get used to the situation. Divorce seems more and more common today. But nothing can replace the need in a child's life to look up and see both parents, always there, full of love for each other and for the child.

I wish we could take back each of our mistakes, but life keeps moving on. We can only share our stories with each other and hope to learn from our mistakes.

SURVIVAL-GUIDE TOOL

TRUST IS TRICKY

Trust is an elusive concept. It can be lost or gained within a single moment. Trust is based on the belief in someone, and if you go into a relationship without it, or if it is somehow damaged, it's a messy road to get back on track.

If you have cheated or been cheated on, you know it isn't easy to regain trust. Even if the person who cheated swears it will never happen again, there's always the doubt in the back of your mind: a hidden text message, a deleted e-mail, or a muffled phone call, and your mind begins to race. The questions never cease. It can be exhausting for both parties.

So, how do you regain trust? First, you have to trust *yourself.* After an affair, you can start to question your own judgment. You wonder if you're even with the right person, if you've missed the obvious signs, if your perception of reality is off, if you're a bad person, if you brought this on yourself, or if you're not good enough. The questions can become exhausting and lead you down an unhealthy path.

You will also have to work with your partner to help him stop lying, being defensive, and placing blame. He must agree to avoid situations that could lead to another relationship, and he must completely cut ties with his lover and be willing to answer your questions about the affair. Remember that there's no timetable for healing. You, your relationship, and your trust in your partner may take a while to recover.

WAYS TO LEAVE YOUR PARTNER

Breaking up is never easy. If you have been cheated on or are suspicious that your partner is cheating, take the following advice first: figure out what you *really* want. This might require some time alone, but ask yourself these hard questions first, before you make any permanent decisions:

1. *What would I do if my partner actually cheated on me?* We often say we will do one thing, but infidelity is not necessarily a deal breaker, especially if you have children or are economically dependent on your spouse.

2. *What would make me happy?* Such a simple question, but one that is often loaded with hidden meanings. What is happiness to you? Do you need some time on your own? Do you already know that you want to break up, but just don't want to be the one to do it? Are you staying in your marriage only for the kids? The stability? The fact that you've been together forever? Figure out what would make you happy, what you want, and then take the necessary steps to get there.

3. *How would I feel if I went through with it? Think about leaving your partner.* Imagine what that would actually mean. Think about the logistical steps: getting a new place to live, hiring a lawyer,

dividing your things, dealing with wishy-washy emotions, regrets, anger. Contemplate what this new reality would be like and how you would handle the changes.

4. What will I do next? Often people act before they think. They will leave a partner and then are forced to come back because they have nowhere to go. However, be wary of overthinking. If you're paralyzed because you don't think you could make it on your own, realize that thousands of women do it every year. Make a plan to get on your own two feet. You simply *make* things work if you want it badly enough.

5. Is he likely to hurt me if I try to leave him? During breakups, emotions run extremely high. Some women stay with men due to the sheer rage and terror inflicted by a loose cannon of a boyfriend or husband. What will he do? Will he come after me? Will he hurt me? Fear can keep people locked in place. Get help before you get out. Talk to someone at a battered women's shelter, enlist trusted friends, and make sure you have a safety plan before you confront him.

Before Confrontation

If you do decide to break up with your partner over infidelity, make sure you have the facts first. Do you know your partner cheated, or do you just suspect it? Are you simply looking for a way out? Are you at your wit's end? Make your decision based on what you want (no matter how hard things get). If you start to waver once you have to fill out paperwork or divide your silverware, then this might not be the right decision for you. Breakups are hard.

Period. So, decide what you want and then stick to it. Being in limbo doesn't help anyone.

If it helps, talk with trusted friends or family members, but don't ask for too many opinions. Often, people are influenced by what their friends or family think. This is a decision between you and your partner. Though it would be easy to have someone tell you what to do, this is only a choice you can make. Sometimes talking about it or analyzing the situation to death just keeps you in a state of inactivity. It's easy to talk about these things and go around in circles.

During Confrontation

Assuming your partner has cheated, or you suspect an affair, emotions will be running rampant. Though you may be irate, sickened, sad, and any emotion in between, it is important to convey exactly what you want. More than likely, your partner will be feeling great remorse and will beg for your forgiveness. This is where your resolve comes into play, and you have to stay strong and make sure you know what you want. Talk in a calm, even tone of voice. State what you want in clear terms. Do not let yourself get angry or defensive. Don't ask why.

UNCOVER
HOW TO MOVE ON AFTER AN AFFAIR

Moving on after an affair is never easy. Now only around 50 percent of married couples say infidelity would be a deal breaker, while a decade ago that number was closer to 90 percent. So, it is evident that people's thoughts about infidelity are shifting, but that doesn't mean moving on after an affair—whether you are staying with your partner or leaving—makes it any easier.

You will be angry, confused, and upset. But know this: anger and hurt fuel you to move forward, to divorce, to separate, and sometimes, to take care of all the things you need to do. In some cases, anger can even lead to forgiveness. However, when things calm down, and you find yourself alone, the hard part settles in. This is what you have to ask yourself: If your partner cheated, can you get past it? Is breaking this vow or promise just as bad as breaking all the other vows? Could you ever trust him again? Can you forgive? If not, then you probably need to move on.

Moving On After Breaking Up

Because moving on is never easy, we have compiled a list of the best ways to move on:

- Distance yourself from the situation. Attempt to take emotions out of it and look at the situation logically.
- Once you have decided who will go or stay, stop or limit communication with the person to what is strictly necessary for legal reasons or to deal with issues regarding children. This means no checking up on him on Facebook, perusing through old texts, or stalking your old haunts hoping to run into him. If you are breaking up, you are breaking up. Force yourself to move on. Don't respond to last-ditch efforts on his part to get you back.
- Make a list of assets that will need to be shared and/or sold and any legalities that need to be taken care of. Find out laws in your state. If you have children, decide on custody issues based on what would be best for your child, not what would be best for your anger.

- Once you leave, don't look back. There is nothing worse than reminiscing or romanticizing a relationship. Move on. Period.
- Do not retaliate. Don't ask questions, and don't offer up information about your personal life or any new love interest. Be as removed as possible, and through this removal, slowly start to rebuild your self-esteem. Remember that affairs are rarely a reflection of *your* shortcomings. It is almost always about the other person and his wants or needs. Cheating is primarily a selfish act, a quick fix for temporary fulfillment. Remembering this will help keep you from retaliating or making any kind of childish, immature mistakes. Will sleeping with someone else *really* make you feel better? Destroying his property? It won't change what happened. It's important to keep moving forward.
- Confide in friends about how you are feeling. It's important to have a solid support group. Start a journal. Scream. Cry. Drink. Eat. Exercise. Make sure you feel something, and don't hold back any emotions, good, bad, or ugly.
- Heal at your own pace. There's no specific amount of time or space that means you're healed, ready to date, or over someone. Every person and every situation is different. Do not rush. If you want to be alone, be alone. If you want to date, date. It's up to you, but remember to take care of yourself. Focus on your specific wants and needs and what you really want out of a relationship.
- Be prepared to lose your resolve. At first, with a breakup, if you are the one initiating it, it's likely you've taken time to think it through. You are relieved that you have *finally* made a decision. But, once you get over that initial "high," reality does set in, and it can be lonely. Anytime you go from being a twosome to being single, it can be completely overwhelming. This is the

time when you have to realize you won't be healed overnight. It takes time, and it's best to deal with each and every emotion as it comes at you, rather than pushing them away, going to clubs, or ignoring them. It's like therapy: the faster you face your issues head on, the quicker you can move on.

- Travel. As cliché as this sounds, it is one of the most rewarding and eye-opening experiences possible. Don't plan. Just go.
- Volunteer. Put yourself in a position to help. As gut-wrenching as affairs are, it can always be worse. Literally. Sometimes helping others puts your own situation into perspective. Go visit a women's shelter, where abused women have been left penniless, with their children in tow. Sitting and talking to one of these women for an hour can put your own life in greater perspective.
- Don't believe that every man you meet will cheat on you. Look at this experience as a learning experience. Don't punish the next person you are in a relationship with because of your partner's past mistakes.
- Acknowledge your own mistakes. It usually takes two people to make a relationship fail. Though you can't "push" someone to have an affair, there are often missing components that make partners want to find these traits in someone else. Take some time to analyze what went right and what went wrong in your relationship so you can avoid making the same mistakes in any future relationships.
- Move on. After you have taken time to dwell, be angry, cry, scream, take up new hobbies, date, be silly, burn photos and mementos, miss the person, feel guilty, have regrets, *move on*. You can't change what happened, no matter how many times you replay details in your head. Don't forget to live your life.

Things happen for a reason. Live and learn. Continue to forge relationships. If and when you find someone new, be clear on your feelings about infidelity and set the stage for clear-cut boundaries. Tell the person up front how you feel and what are non-negotiable areas for you. Make sure you don't ever put yourself in the same situation again.

Moving On While Staying Together

If you decide to stay with your partner despite an affair, realize you can't keep him on a leash twenty-four hours a day. You have to learn to fall in love again, to rebuild trust, and that will take time. You can't constantly use the affair as a Band-Aid. You have to be willing to accept this mistake, and move past it. This is not an easy endeavor, but if you decide your relationship is worth it, it's up to you how to proceed. Here are some tips:

1. Don't be concerned with what family members or friends might think of your decision. Choosing to stay with a partner who has cheated is a completely personal choice. It is a brave thing to do—to keep your relationship together—and will take work and trust. It is your life, no one else's.

2. Don't punish your partner. Let him talk about it if he needs to, and decide what it is you need to know about the affair to reconcile it in your head. Do you need to know details? Then be prepared to hear them. Would you rather forget that it ever happened? Then you can't let yourself bring it up, especially if you are fighting or things aren't going your way. Again, take some time to decide what will be best for you, and then talk about it.

3. Keep the lines of communication open. Discover how the affair happened in the first place. Had you grown distant with your partner? Crazy work hours? Discover how you can get that romance back, even if it takes time.

4. Rebuild your self-esteem. It is easy to blame yourself if you were cheated on. You feel like you aren't enough, physically or mentally. Find ways to validate yourself and feel good, and don't always look to your partner to give you this validation. Insecurities of any kind are hard to live with, and you can't expect your partner to constantly eradicate these insecurities. Take time to work on yourself. Confidence is sexy.

5. Learn to like your partner again. You must learn to *like* each other again, not just love each other. You are going to be with this person for a long time. You better start finding traits you appreciate. If you weren't together, would you value this person as a friend? If the answer is no, find out how you can become better friends.

6. Become friends with your partner. Perhaps you are friends, or were friends, or perhaps you were never really friends. Now is the time to forge a friendship or rebuild one. Often, when people are in relationships, they have a different set of rules and tolerances for their significant other than they would for their friends. Do you ever notice how you even *listen* differently when your best friend is telling you a story, versus when your partner is? Couples are often too quick to judge each other, instead of being open. Try it. Be open and receptive. Don't judge.

7. Rediscover what you love about your partner. Remember in the beginning when you were infatuated? Falling in love over and over again with the same person is key for a long-lasting relationship. Focus on what you love about each other.

8. Learn to forgive. There is no point in holding grudges. If you are staying with someone after an affair, you have to forgive him completely. It is the only way you will get past it. Forgiving someone of an affair versus forgiving someone for accidentally breaking a dish may seem like two separate things. But there are no degrees of forgiveness. Forgiving someone for a minor offense or a big offense is all the same. If you have truly decided to stay with your partner, you must be able to forgive. Everyone is human, and everyone makes mistakes. Some mistakes are larger than others, but everyone is susceptible.

9. Believe what your partner tells you. Sometimes it's so easy to spin an idea of what you think happened, instead of what *actually* happened. It is possible to live and learn, and just because someone cheated once does not mean he will do it again.

10. Become more social. Taking up new interests after an affair can give you a sense of confidence. Sometimes you get so caught up in your own little world and relationships, you forget what's outside of your self-constructed bubbles. Travel, see the world, volunteer. Take some time for yourself, and realize that not everything has to be shared with your partner. Having something that is yours and yours alone—a passion of sorts—can help your relationship.

11. Seek professional counseling. Sometimes it feels good to talk to an objective person outside of your social circle who can give you some sound advice.

12. Be patient. While time won't change what happened, it does make things easier. Take it a single day at a time, and don't get impatient. This too shall pass.

13. Make adjustments in your relationship. Why did this happen in the first place? Not enough time spent together, not enough attraction, not enough sex? You must make the proper adjustments so you can improve the relationship and keep each other satisfied. It is a two-way street.

14. Be honest. Honesty means you trust each other enough to tell the truth, without hassling each other or saying, "I don't believe you." You have to trust each other to be honest. And the only way you can have honesty is to provide a loving, open, nondefensive environment where both of you can communicate and feel safe enough to be completely forthcoming with even the smallest concern.

15. Laugh together. If you can find ways to laugh and play, you can learn to trust and love again. It truly is that simple.

HOW DO YOU KNOW WHEN YOU SHOULD STAY TOGETHER?

If your partner has cheated and you are torn between staying to work it out or leaving, how do you decide? Asking the following questions may help:

1. Is this the first offense?
   A. I don't care enough to know anymore. Once is too much
   B. No
   C. Still not sure
   D. Yes

2. What kind of affair was it?
   A. They had sex many times
   B. They had sex once
   C. They kissed but that's as far as it went
   D. It was only an emotional affair. Nothing physical happened

3. How long did the affair last?
   A. Years
   B. A few months
   C. A few weeks
   D. It was a one-night stand

4. Are you still in love with your partner?
   A. No
   B. Yes, but I'm not sure I can trust him again
   C. I'm not sure
   D. Yes

5. Does your partner show remorse about the infidelity?
   A. No
   B. At times, but he becomes defensive and tends to switch blame
   C. He has apologized but his actions don't match it
   D. Yes, he has been completely supportive

6. Does your partner have a history of infidelity?
   A. Yes, my partner has cheated in his past relationship(s) many times
   B. Yes, my partner has cheated in his past relationship(s) at least once
   C. I don't know
   D. No, my partner never cheated in his past relationship(s)

7. Are you ready to split up because of the infidelity?
   A. Yes, I am so over this
   B. No, but only if things change and this never happens again
   C. I'm not sure
   D. No, absolutely not. I want to keep trying to move forward

8. Did your partner continue to lie to you when you found out?
   A. Yes, he denied it until the end
   B. Yes, but as time passed more and more truthful details emerged
   C. No, but he was unwilling to tell me what happened unless pressured
   D. No, he was honest and told me everything

9. Is your partner in love with the other person?
   A. Yes
   B. No, he said it was just physical
   C. I'm not sure
   D. No, my partner is still in love with me

ANSWER KEY

Mostly A's: This relationship is pretty much over and it's time for you to move on. The lying and unwillingness to move forward will prevent healing and the process of regaining trust. Patience, regaining trust, and time are the names of the healing game, and this relationship doesn't seem to have any of those things. As difficult as it may be, it might be time for you to explore moving on.

Mostly B's: Whether your relationship survives really depends on whether you believe there is anything worth saving in the relationship. Besides the infidelity, is your partner a loving partner, a good parent, a hard worker, trustworthy, and your best friend? If you answered yes to these questions, this relationship may be worth saving. But, you will have to repair trust and move forward one step at a time.

Mostly C's: You aren't sure if you will stay or go. If you still don't know if you want to continue in your relationship, you may need to give it some more time. It is perfectly natural to feel betrayed, hurt, and disappointed after an affair. You may not be able to think rationally during this time when you are still processing your emotions. You may need some time apart to process it all before you make your decision. Don't put any pressure on yourself or rush into a decision. Take the time you need in order to make the right decision for yourself and your circumstances.

Mostly D's: Give it a try. There still seems to be love and willingness to make this relationship work. You seem to have genuine love and empathy between the two of you, so if you work together, you have a good chance of repairing the damage. It's important to keep communication open in order to prevent this from happening again. Everyone is human, and everyone makes mistakes. Learn to forgive as you would want to be forgiven, and see how your relationship progresses.

CHAPTER ELEVEN

"Making Your Relationship Affair-Proof"

"Being happy doesn't mean that everything is perfect. It means that you've decided to look beyond the imperfections."

—ANONYMOUS

Though we've discussed the realities of infidelity, there *are* ways to prevent your partner from straying. All partnerships take constant re-evaluating and checking in to make sure physical and emotional needs are being met. It's normal to have changing needs and desires, and it is possible to keep those wants in line with your partner's. An open line of communication and appreciation go a long way in setting the stage to make your relationship affair-proof. Fidelity can be fulfilling if you learn to stay proactive about issues in your relationship and recognize that all relationships require hard work and constant attention.

Relationships are tricky. In the beginning, you are deep in the throes of passion, of falling for all of the traits you adore about the other person. The honeymoon stage passes, and the idiosyncrasies sink in, but you ignore them until you realize that what was at first endearing is now irritating. Without realizing it, you subconsciously get a taste of compromise and realize the hidden meaning in the phrase "choose your battles wisely."

Despite these new developments, you get engaged or married anyway. You assume that all couples fight (true) and that the newness can't last forever (false), and you become annoyed and short-tempered; you long for something you had in the beginning of your relationship that seems lost or buried.

Well, guess what? It's not simply about reminding yourself why you are with your partner—you have to feel it too. Revisiting those emotions from the start of your relationship is a great way to reintroduce the intimacy to your relationship. It's easy to fall prey to the woes of stress and exhaustion, but it is up to the both of you to dictate the terms of your relationship. Romantic relationships take work. If and when you find yourself worn down by nagging, exhaustion, or constant frustration, do the following:

1. Remember back to a specific day or time when you felt irrevocably in love. What were you doing? What were the circumstances? Had you and your partner just started dating? Were you free of obligations? Try to re-create a night or situation that reminds you of those intense feelings. Play a familiar song, make a familiar meal . . . the important thing is to revive your senses.

2. Don't set unrealistic expectations. In the beginning, everyone imagines her life will always be filled with health and happiness. But happiness sometimes falters, and plans don't always work out as hoped. For instance, if a couple gets married and wants a child, but that doesn't happen, they can become obsessed with what they can't or don't have, and in turn, lose their connection with each other. Make sure that nothing takes the focus off the importance of your relationship and staying together. It's essential that you're with each other because you really want to be and truly like each other (just as important as loving each other)—not because you want to live out a dream that may not go as planned. Be with someone you can talk to, listen to, someone who complements your lifestyle.

3. Be intimate. Always be intimate. This can be through holding hands, kissing softly, rubbing your partner's back, etc. Have a physical connection with your partner, and make sure you stay affectionate. In an instant, it can change how you feel about a situation and bring a sense of lightness and ease to your day.

4. Be generous. It's so nice to surprise your partner with a gift, a handwritten letter, dinner, a trip, etc. Be spontaneous, and think about what would make your partner feel good. Sometimes when a woman is in a relationship she focuses on herself—what she's not getting, what he isn't doing, etc. Instead, focus on how you can make your partner feel good, and show him tiny tokens of appreciation along the way.

5. Play. Joke. Laugh. Get in a wrestling match. Be goofy. Just because you're an adult, it doesn't mean you have to be serious all the time. A lot of times, people think that just because they have adult responsibilities, the fun is over. Couples have a house, kids, and money woes. . . . But that does not mean they should stop having fun or take each other for granted. Everyone is young at heart. Start a pillow fight. Create a simple treasure hunt in the bedroom. Chase your partner in a grocery store. Make up a new romantic nickname. Laugh. Tickle each other. Do something unexpected and fun.

Think about the small things you can do to make your relationship better, and remember to take it a day at a time.

SURVIVAL-GUIDE TOOL
A MARRIAGE EXAMINED

People often cheat because of something missing in the relationship. By paying attention to your relationship, you make it less likely that your partner will seek to find rewards outside of it.

The following questionnaire should help you think of ways to improve your relationship to make it less susceptible to infidelity. Take the time to study and answer each question. If your partner is willing, take the quiz together, with each of you writing your answers on a separate piece of paper. Crack open a bottle of wine, put on some music, and share your answers. Create a comfortable, distraction-free environment where the two of you can talk openly. Pinpoint the biggest issues in your relationship and the smaller, everyday issues. Breaking them down into fixable problems can go a long way in repairing a broken marriage, or at least figuring out the next step.

1. What is missing in your current relationship? Have you suddenly lost the passion? Does your partner not listen to you? Are you both exhausted? Do you not feel "desire" for your partner? Do you find yourself annoyed? Do you find yourself nagging all the time? Have you become resentful of your life? Is the intimacy gone? Do you find yourself wanting different things? Pinpointing what is missing can help you figure out what you both want and need for a successful union.

2. What attracted you to your partner? Remember what you loved about your partner in the beginning. Make a list of the top five traits that you found so attractive. Are these traits still evident? Can you still see them? Try to focus on this list for a specific period of time. When you find yourself pointing out something negative, see if you can replace it with a positive thought.

3. When do you get annoyed or fight? Do you fight when you are tired, hungry, or when you feel like you need something else . . . something more? Find out if you are fighting for a legitimate reason (he disrespects you or calls you names, for instance) or for a minor reason (he forgot to pick his laundry up off the floor). Divide your issues into manageable ones (household chores) and more serious ones, like a lack of respect or romance, and see which ones you can tackle head on.

4. Do you depend on your significant other for everything? A companion shouldn't have to satisfy all the voids in your life. You cannot place your every desire on one person. Think about realistic expectations for both of you.

5. Do you ever fantasize about someone new? If you find yourself fantasizing about a new person, realize it's just that: *a fantasy.* Fantasies really should stay in your head, unless you are truly unhappy. If you are truly unhappy, break up with the person before you act on foolish impulses. If you are married, talk to your partner or see a counselor. No one deserves to be cheated on. Remember that *every* relationship requires work and compromise. You are with your current partner for a reason. Try to remember those reasons and try reconnecting.

6. What traits are you attracted to in other people? If you ever find yourself drawn to someone else, notice why. Is it the newness? Does this person have a passion that you admire, or do you have common interests? Did you recognize these same traits in your partner when you first met? Realize that this excitement about someone new will most likely fade, just like it did with your original partner. Try to pinpoint exactly where the attraction is and see if you can't remedy what's missing in your current relationship.

If you cannot stop thinking about someone else, play out the affair in your head. See it through. Think about the logistics. The guilt. The lies. The betrayal. It's never as simple as sex. Emotions, feelings, and complications always get involved, and affairs are *never* worth it in the end. If you are unhappy, say you are unhappy. Don't use an attraction to someone else as a crutch to cover up the shortcomings in your own relationship.

7. What's great about your relationship? For one week, try to focus exclusively on *your* relationship. Not what you wish you had or you wish was different, but *your* relationship, flaws and all. Focus on what's right in the union. Notice all the little quirks and routines you have, and what's special about your union. It takes much less effort to focus on what's good than constantly being annoyed about what's wrong. Give it a real effort. If you do make an honest effort to focus on your relationship and your issues aren't going away, talk to your partner about it, no matter how uncomfortable or hard it is. It's better to talk about these things than make stupid, rash decisions or look elsewhere for answers. Always communicate your concerns, and give your partner the room to do the same.

8. Are you still attracted to your partner? Attraction hinges upon more than looks. If you disrespect your partner or are disrespected, if you feel unwanted or unappreciated, attraction can shift. Before blurting out, "I am not attracted to you anymore," or "I'm attracted to someone else," figure out why your attraction level has changed. If you decide to address the issue, figure out a way to phrase it so your partner will not get defensive. To reignite that spark, take your partner off guard by kissing him passionately while he's doing something mundane. Throw yourself at him and drop whatever you're doing to mix things up. See if the spark is still there.

9. Are you exhausted? If the problem is being too busy with work or dealing with the demands of kids, understand that these issues will exist no matter *who* you're with. If you are in a long-term relationship, you will go through lulls. Make sure that you are both doing all you can to help the other person when it comes to chores/responsibilities at home. Find a way to separate a real lack of connection with mere day-to-day chores. Connect in small ways: if you know you are going to be exhausted at the end of the night, take five minutes and have a make-out session with your partner right when you walk in the door. Little gestures like this go a long way. Think about small gestures you can do in your own relationship that might add up.

10. *If you could change anything about your partner, what would it be?* If you could change anything about your relationship? If you could change anything about yourself? Really ponder these questions, and see what changes are possible. For instance, if you hate how your partner treats you, or you both nag at each other, this is something that can change. If you can't stand the way he laughs or that he snores or that his back is hairy, these are traits that will most likely not change, but they shouldn't be deal breakers either. Look at issues that will make a real, long-term difference.

11. *Can you imagine yourself living without your partner?* What would your life be like? Both of you take some time to really think about the logistics, the day-to-day, the struggles and possible new challenges. Do you still want to be a team, or are you both truly unhappy? Focus on ways to satisfy both of your needs.

SURVIVAL-GUIDE TOOL
WHY MEN CHEAT

You've heard the excuses that fall from the lips of guilty parties: "It just happened." "I wasn't thinking." "It's not you; it's me." "I am in love with someone else." People cheat for numerous reasons. Traditionally, men cheat for physical reasons and women cheat for emotional reasons, but these stereotypes aren't necessarily true. Here are some of the most popular excuses cheaters use to justify their affairs:

Boredom
ANTIDOTE: If you're feeling bored, chances are, he is too. When he becomes bored, fantasies can start to develop. To prevent bore-

dom from becoming a reason for him to start an affair, take steps. Figure out *what* is boring. Is it your routine, the fact that you do the same things every day? The fact that you don't see each other and when you do, you discuss tasks and chores? Tired of making dinner and sitting on the couch watching TV? Turn off the TV and take a walk. Turn on music, open a bottle of wine, and talk about your day. Find a way to laugh. Take up a new hobby. Go to a comedy show. Do something new to shake up your routine. Talk about something completely different. If you are normally the talker, listen. If you are the listener, speak up. Try to rediscover what's great about your relationship and pinpoint what is boring so you can fix it.

Money

ANTIDOTE: People get married for money, they divorce for money, and they even stay in unhappy relationships for money. This kind of unhappiness can make an affair seem to be an attractive distraction. If you don't have enough money, stop focusing on what you don't have and figure out creative ways to bring in more income together. Putting all the monetary pressure on one person puts undue stress on a relationship. If your partner is the breadwinner, make sure you are putting in your own efforts, whether that be at home, paying special attention to your partner's needs, helping him relax, etc. If one of you is in charge of the finances, sit down with the other and try to make it more of a team effort. Make budgets. Talk openly about money, but don't put all the emphasis on money. While money can provide freedom, it can also provide an enormous amount of stress. Happiness in your relationship should not be tied to money in any direct way. Make sure you steer clear of this trap and focus on what you do have, which extends far beyond a bank balance.

Desire for Adventure

ANTIDOTE: Some people feel trapped, bored, or too safe, as though their lives have become distant versions of what they once thought they should be. People need to feel excitement in their lives, and oftentimes they get that excitement outside their marriage. If your partner doesn't feel special or wanted, he may be susceptible to someone who takes an interest in him. Make sure your partner feels wanted.

Do you even look at your partner—really look at him anymore? Do you take time to notice his body, to slow down and savor the moment? Oftentimes, what we want can be achieved with what we have, but we are so used to looking for the next great thing. See if you can attain that sense of rebellion in your own union without looking anywhere else. For instance, make sure you have something exciting that you look forward to, whether that's a hobby, a sexual escapade in an unusual place, or a trip. Figure out what you and your partner need to feel satisfied and make sure to get it.

Your partner can't read your mind. If you want to feel adored, tell him. Give him the chance to do something romantic or off-the-wall. If you just want to experience a change of scenery, go to a club or on vacation and throw caution to the wind. Just because you have responsibilities does not mean you can't have fun. Find ways to have everything you want.

Low Self-Esteem

ANTIDOTE: If your partner feels insecure or worthless, he's more likely to stray. But insecurity is tricky. If *you* are insecure, you're more likely to think he's straying even if he's not. You need to be on equal footing with your partner. If your partner is insecure, be complimentary and help him build up self-esteem. Be sure you're not tearing him down. Treat him with respect and give him compliments. Encourage him to try new things and go after what he really wants. This can help boost his self-confidence and lead to feeling worthwhile. If your partner feels worthless in your own relationship, it is easy for him to seek comfort in someone else (and vice versa).

If your partner gives you compliments all the time, don't brush them off. Acknowledge compliments and thank your partner. Believe your partner when he tells you you're attractive. See how that might change the way you interact with him.

Neglect

ANTIDOTE: Not getting enough attention is one reason people justify affairs. If your partner isn't getting enough emotional or physical attention or sex, he may decide to get it somewhere else, or even develop emotional connections to fill that void. Many times, when men are not getting enough emotional attention, they will innocently find it somewhere else, which frequently leads to physical infidelity.

Find time to connect with your partner. Physically, make sure you touch and hug and kiss. Intimacy does not always mean sex. If it's emotional neglect, make sure you are emotionally invested in your partner (and vice versa). Sometimes people can have "selective listening," or just be exhausted and want to zone out. This can lead to emotional frigidity and feelings of neglect. Keep an open line of communication with your partner, and make sure you are both being fulfilled.

Lack of Respect

ANTIDOTE: Everyone needs respect—men especially. If men feel emasculated or talked down to, they can strike back by embarking on an affair. Show him how much you care by complimenting him—on his job, his looks, his intelligence, his humor, or his wit. Make him feel secure and wanted. If you are the one who lacks respect, try to tell your partner exactly how you feel, but without getting defensive or calling names.

Find small ways to build up that trust and respect. Compliments, acknowledgement, and appreciation go a long way toward making your relationship affair-proof. And when you are in a relationship, it's supposed to be positive. Otherwise, what's the point? It's supposed to be based on love and happiness, so try to be nicer to the one you are with.

Revenge

ANTIDOTE: When a partner feels wronged in a relationship (whether due to lack of respect, because lines were crossed, or as a result of an affair), he can sometimes seek revenge by having an affair. Be careful in how you convey concerns and criticisms. "If you weren't so out of shape, I might want to sleep with you!" may be true, but it's the kind of attack that could send your partner looking for a way to prove that not everyone thinks he's out of shape. If you have to come clean about something you've done, make sure you're ready to deal with the fallout, and consider the possible consequences.

Emotional Detachment

ANTIDOTE: Feeling emotionally detached in a relationship can cause your partner to seek that emotional connection elsewhere. If you're feeling some distance in your relationship, have a conversation about it. Ask if he feels something is missing, or how you can make the relationship more enjoyable. Find ways to improve your connection. For instance, if your partner walks through the door in a bad mood, you could get frustrated if you are ready to have a nice, fun evening. But, did you ask why he is upset or help assuage the situation? Maybe your partner doesn't want to talk right when he walks through the door, so if you can find ways to give each other space and attention, it can forge the way to a deeper emotional connection. It's not all about you, and it's not all about him. It's about both of your needs, equally. Try to find the balance.

Co-dependence

ANTIDOTE: If your partner feels you rely too heavily on him for everything, it can feel like a suffocating trap—and an affair can seem like an attractive outlet. If you've never been alone or are afraid of being alone or look to your partner for absolutely everything—the physical, emotional, mental, and spiritual connection—you're putting a lot of pressure on him. It's important to have a life outside of your relationship and depend on yourself first. Take steps toward becoming more independent. Take on more responsibilities so your roles are more equal.

Thrill of the Chase

ANTIDOTE: When you get too settled at home, nothing seems like a challenge anymore (besides getting along, maybe). Some people like the challenge, the thrill of seeking new attention or getting compliments from someone else. It's an ego boost. Set up this "thrill of the chase" within your own union. Play hard to get. Don't be too predictable. Shake things up in the bedroom. Instead of staying in and making dinner, surprise your partner with a scavenger hunt where he must find clues to discover the final destination. Have fun with your partner. A marriage or committed relationship can still have that thrill—you just have to make a commitment to keeping things exciting. Also be realistic. While it's nice to have a thrill, no one's relationship is constantly stimulating. Real relationships have their quiet moments, their tough moments, and their beautiful moments. If it's the right union, all of those can be thrilling too.

A Sense of Entitlement

ANTIDOTE: Some men simply think they are entitled to do what they want. They see nothing wrong with having someone at home and someone on the side. Men with money often feel a sense of entitlement to do what they want, when they want, with no regard to consequences. If you are in this position, remind your partner that you are together for a reason. Tell your partner that you feel he does not think about the consequences of his behaviors or actions. Sometimes this sense of entitlement is hard to break. Make yourself a little less available to your partner. Don't cater to his every need. Make him think about someone other than himself for a change. Remind him that there are two people in the relationship, and you are both entitled to be happy.

Unhappiness

ANTIDOTE: "Happiness" is a tricky concept. What *is* happiness? A steady paycheck? Having a lot of money? Seven hundred friends on Facebook? An adrenaline rush? Being physically attractive or having a partner who is physically attractive? Traveling?

Being happy with yourself is one of the most important tips to being happy in a relationship. Working on yourself is only fair before you can expect to work on someone else. Ever notice how sometimes you project your own insecurities on someone else? Do most of your sentences begin with "I need, I feel, I want"? If so, you might need to re-evaluate what happiness means in terms of yourself and *then* in the context of a relationship. No one is happy all the time. Relationships take constant push and pull. Learn how to push and pull, and give and take.

There needs to be a balance. If you are too focused on making your partner happy (or vice versa), your own happiness can be left by the wayside. Look at the term *happiness* from everyone's point of view so you can find ways to ultimate satisfaction in your union.

Not Enough Sex

ANTIDOTE: Sex makes everything better. It's a known fact that if you are getting enough sex at home, you are less inclined to look for it elsewhere. (Hint: if he enjoys sex and he's not getting it, he's bound to get it somewhere else.) That being said, define what a good amount of sex is for *your* relationship. Don't think of it as a chore. Sure, it can get monotonous, but make a rule that sex, much like eating or paying bills or working, is a priority. It's a part of your relationship—don't let that slip away.

Think of it as yet another way you can connect with your partner. It doesn't have to be a big production. Be spontaneous. Be quick. Be passionate. Sex doesn't always have to be sex—it can be foreplay, using your hands, or your mouth. Mix it up and always try to keep that spark alive. Have sex first thing in the morning, stop by the office for an afternoon session, or send him sexy messages all day long. Men like to be taken by surprise. Make the move on him, and you might be surprised how his passion becomes not about sex, but about you.

Sexual Curiosity

ANTIDOTE: People are curious. They can get bored with the same partner, the same positions, and the same sexual experiences. It's human nature. Consider ways to spice up your sex life. Is something missing in your current relationship? Can you improve your sex life by watching porn, role-playing, or talking dirty together? See what you can do within your union to get that spark back. But remember, you have to be open and talk about it. Don't be embarrassed and don't get mad at him if he says he would like you to talk dirty, role-play, watch porn, or try something new sexually. Instead of dismissing the idea, be receptive. You might surprise yourself and him.

To Re-experience Feelings of Romance

ANTIDOTE: The beginning of a relationship can often be the most intense and romantic. As time passes and you build more into your life (jobs, kids, pets, and mortgages) life stressors can take over and the romance falls to the wayside. Think about romance in simple ways. Making a candlelit dinner. Drawing a picture. Leaving little notes before work. Flowers. Music. Taking a walk while holding hands. Find ways to surprise your partner and bring back a little romance every day. The gesture is often what it is all about.

To Feel Wanted and Needed

ANTIDOTE: Everyone wants to feel desired. In the beginning of a relationship, it's easy to feel wanted. But, with time, you can become consumed by tasks and other to-dos and you or your partner can become neglected or neglectful. Are you still attracted to your partner? Do you still desire him? If not, why? Attraction is vital for long-term commitments. Do you need more attention? Do you need to give more attention? Talk to your partner openly and see what both of you need and how you can make each other feel more desired.

Loneliness

ANTIDOTE: There is nothing worse than being with someone and still feeling lonely. Relationships take constant care and upkeep. You can't just assume your partner knows how much you love him and that's that. You have to like each other, spend time together, cater to each other's needs, compromise, communicate, and deal with money, stress, family, selfishness, exhaustion, and much more.

Being supportive and present are vital. It's easy to be in a relationship and just go through the motions because you feel like you have no other choice. Do you still like your partner? Do you like who you are with your partner? Why are you lonely? Are you lonely at night or during the day? Do you feel lonely when you're away from your partner or sitting right next to him? Communicate your concerns. Cuddle at night. Watch a movie together. Instead of eating dinner in front of the television, take time to sit across from each other and actually discuss your day. Make eye contact. Have a real conversation. Have a laughing attack. Become friends again.

Lack of Communication

ANTIDOTE: This one is tough. If you constantly feel like you are talking to a closed door, try writing a letter. Sometimes those who aren't good with verbal words are better reading and writing them. Find a way in which your partner is willing to communicate. Make sure (if you are going to have a serious conversation) that you are thinking about making the other person comfortable and approaching him/her in a way that won't cause him to be defensive. Make it known that his feelings are appreciated and respected. Feeling comfortable is key to having open conversations. If he is unhappy, he owes it to you to talk about it. Gently remind him of this and that you want to work on whatever is missing.

Feel Like Roommates

ANTIDOTE: "We're like roommates" is a sentence commonly uttered by those in long-term relationships. The easiest explanation is that you begin to take each other for granted. You know every movement, every gesture, every piece of laundry on the floor, every dirty dish, every annoying thing that you try to ignore. You get into ruts and routines.

It's easy to go out into the world and converse and be genuinely interested in people you don't really know. However, you have to bring that same appreciation home with you. Take comfort that you do have someone to go home to and cook with and snuggle up to. Life is short. It can be cruel and unusual and love is often so tangled with little resentments, you don't even see how beautiful and effortless it could be if you stripped away a little of the baggage.

Telling your partner how much you appreciate him can alter the mood drastically. Find ways to make your home life more enticing. Start small. Focus on one little thing you can do to make your relationship different from a roommate situation every single day. Remember that this person you are living with is more than just a person who completes chores, pays bills, works, eats, and sleeps. You both have interesting thoughts, dreams, and fantasies. Focus more on who you are rather than all the things you must do or get done on a daily basis.

UNCOVER

TIPS FOR A CHEAT-FREE RELATIONSHIP

Psychologists say that the keys to successful relationships are communication, honesty, and compromise. These are all tips we have heard before—but *then* what? We gathered advice from real people who've affair-proofed their relationships. Here are their tips for keeping your relationship cheat-free:

1. Sex, sex, and more sex. The consensus is absolute: Have *a lot* of sex with your partner. *Always* make time for sex. Don't ever look at sex like a chore. Look at it as an opportunity to connect with your partner, to have fun. Keep it interesting and always a priority; don't ever withhold sex or act like it's a privilege or a rare occasion.
2. Laugh. Every single day.
3. Share household chores. Evenly.
4. Think about monogamy as an exciting prospect: you don't have to worry about sexually transmitted diseases; you don't have to play games; and you can explore, change, and grow with one person and just be yourself.
5. *Like* your partner, don't just love him.
6. Learn everything about your partner, especially his likes and dislikes. Go beyond the physical. Get to know him on a

mental and emotional level and don't be afraid to tell him what you like and don't like. Let fears and pleasures be known at all times, because things change at different times in your life.

7. Three words: separate checking accounts.

8. Just stick with the person that makes you not want anyone else.

9. Respect your partner. Respect yourself. Respect the boundaries between you.

10. Hold hands while you are fighting. It is almost impossible to stay angry.

11. Tell your partner one thing you appreciate about him every day.

12. Be secure. Insecurities are often a breeding ground for infidelity.

13. Don't create drama.

14. Never stop playing.

15. You have to truly love yourself in order to love someone else to your full potential.

16. Be with the person for the right reasons, not because he has a good job or makes money. If that quality is gone, what will sustain you? Make sure your love is based on something substantial and not materialistic.

17. Remind each other that you can do anything. Focus on what your partner does *right* for a change, of all that he is capable of.

18. Connect right when you get home from the day. Don't wait until you are tired or right before bed to make love.

19. Go on dates. Often.

20. Make more time for each other. Notice how you spend around eight hours of each day working and reserve a mere hour or two to do enjoyable things like exercise, cook, or hang out with your significant other? Try to squeeze more time out of your day for the person who means the most to you.

21. Don't ever let money dictate what you can and can't do in a relationship. The funny thing about money? It's just paper. It shouldn't rule the world or your happiness.

22. If you go out and find yourself flirting, leave it at that. It's natural to flirt, but the responsibility of being in a relationship is that you go home. Be happy to go home to the love of your life.

23. Why does one vagina or penis have to be limiting? Sex is sex, no matter who it's with. Be thankful that you have someone to be with. Appreciate that.

24. Keep it exciting. Find out what your partner's fantasies are and then tell him yours. Don't be afraid to get adventurous and get out of your comfort zone.

25. Don't get annoyed. Ever notice how in the beginning of a relationship, you are riveted to what the other person has to say? You can't take your eyes off of him, your heart beats faster, and you adore everything about him? And then, once time passes and that initial "newness" wears off, all those cute, quirky traits go out the window and you begin to find yourself annoyed? It doesn't have to be like that, so focus on what you love about the person. Don't bring him down or be negative.

26. Don't ever complain about your partner to other people, especially people you are attracted to.

27. Listen. Listen. Listen.

28. Talk. Talk. Talk.

29. Be friends. Make sure you are growing and learning together and not leading totally separate lives. The idea of being with someone is that you actually enjoy his company. It's good to have individual goals and friends outside the relationship, but make sure your partner is one of the best friends you will ever have.

30. Realize that there will always be temptation out there. If you can figure out how you would handle it *before* it happens, you are more likely to remain faithful.

31. Don't set unrealistic demands on each other.

32. Don't get defensive. If you are having a disagreement, approach your partner like you would your best friend. Do you get defensive or yell at your best friend? Probably not. Relax. Be open. Listen to what the other person is trying to say.

33. Don't assume you know how your partner will react. "He's too judgmental; she doesn't understand me." Give him the benefit of the doubt.

34. Know that marriage is harder than raising kids, and that you will have to work at it. But you should want to work at it because you love each other.

35. Always appreciate each other and find little ways to show that appreciation.

36. Find newness with your partner every day. Find some new trait you haven't noticed or some beautiful quality.

37. Celebrate your differences. Don't dwell on them.

38. Love is the glue, but all of the other little things you have in common matter the most for a lasting relationship.

39. Don't ever say "I love you" without feeling it.

40. Don't fight when you are tired or hungry.

41. Don't go to bed angry.

42. Realize that if he's not getting sex and you're not getting an emotional connection, you are both likely to look for it elsewhere.

43. Look for what you're not getting within your own relationship first.

44. Don't depend on your partner for absolutely everything. It's not fair to either of you.

45. Always tell the other person what's bothering you. A huge downfall of many relationships is all the little resentments that build up over time. Resolve this by being proactive and being as open as possible.

46. Make it a rule never to call each other names. This sounds easy, but in the heat of the moment, it's easy to say, "You're such an asshole." "You're a bitch." "I hate you." Words are damaging, and people often say what they mean while arguing. No matter how angry you are, do not cross this line. This is how bad habits form.

47. Even if you have totally different interests or careers, come up with something that is just yours and your partner's. Maybe that's a hobby like a sport, a game, sitting outside reading poetry to each other, or hosting a dinner party. Just have something that is both of yours that you look forward to and can share together.

ROLE-PLAYING GUIDE

Role-playing can spice up your love life. This doesn't have to mean elaborate costumes or in-depth acting skills. The entire purpose of role-playing is to free inhibitions and just *let go*. Sex is a time to let go. All day we have one giant to-do list. We are so busy running around, we rarely take the time to slow down, breathe, and enjoy the sensation of kissing or touching. Sometimes we even turn sex into a chore—sex, one of the most enjoyable exercises on the planet. Who doesn't want an orgasm at the end of a stressful day? Start thinking of your "alone" time with your partner as time to have fun, unwind, and really connect.

- One of the most arousing (and easiest) roles to play is playing hard to get. A little resisting will up the sexual desire, and it requires no costumes or feeling uncomfortable. Make your partner work for your affection. The moment he touches you, pull away. Kiss without using your hands. Have fun with foreplay, lasting as long as you can before you finally give in.

- If your partner has a fantasy or fetish and you usually don't give in, try it. This doesn't mean doing something that makes you uncomfortable, but being open to something your partner really wants or enjoys will go a long way. And the old adage is true: you never know if you'll like it until you try it.

- If you are normally the aggressive one, be submissive (and vice versa). Accepting each other for your likes and dislikes, while maintaining proper boundaries of respect, can allow for a uniquely fulfilling experience. If you are the one being aggressive, tie your partner up. Show up naked and take control. Don't let your partner talk. Or, if you are normally the aggressive one, take more of the passive role and let your partner shine.

- Create an exciting experience with an intimate setting. First of all, choose a scenario that is exciting or hot to both of you. Is one of you an artist? Get nude and let him trace the lines of your body. Enjoy feeling vulnerable. Enjoy feeling attractive. Enjoy being studied and admired. Let your partner take advantage of you once he is done, and relish in that feeling of doing something bad.

The bottom line is to do something different—something that doesn't have to include fancy costumes. A little variety goes a long way, especially over a long-term relationship.

TEN WAYS TO SPICE UP YOUR LOVE LIFE

1. Have sex in a new location.
2. Sleep outside under the stars.
3. Give each other massages.
4. Go skinny-dipping together.
5. Take a bubble bath together.
6. Surprise your partner with some sexy new lingerie and let him take it off of you.
7. Go dancing together.
8. Read erotic poetry together.
9. Take turns blindfolding each other during sex and take your time exploring your partner's entire body.
10. Write a sexy text or e-mail to increase the anticipation for sex.

Resources

By now you should know the signs to look for to nail a cheating partner. You have learned all the tips and tricks to make your relationship affair-proof and how to sustain a relationship even after infidelity. The following is a resource list for different services and websites that might help you on your journey. We wish you all the best of luck and many years of fidelity!

CATCHING A CHEATER

www.womansavers.com
Free date-screening service that allows women to research their date's relationship history to make smarter and safer dating decisions.

www.intelius.com
For background checks, verifications, and information services.

www.familywatchdog.us
National sex offender registry.

www.criminalcheck.com
Free national sex offender database.

www.tracerservices.com
Information searches, bug sweeps.

www.infidelitytoday.com
Infidelity test kit that detects traces of semen left in undergarments after sex.

www.cheater-busters.com
GPS vehicle tracking system.

www.spyzone.com
Equipment for video and audio surveillance, tap detection and scrambling, bug detection, bulletproof products, voice stress analysis, audio recording devices, GPS surveillance.

www.thespystore.com
World's largest selection of spy and surveillance equipment.

www.polygraphnow.com
Lie detector testing.

www.pcpandora.com
Key-logging software that records every computer keystroke.

PHYSICAL AND SEXUAL ABUSE HELP

National Domestic Violence Hotline for Abused Women
www.ndvh.org or 1-800-799-SAFE (7233)

RESOURCES

National Teen Dating Abuse Helpline
www.loveisrespect.org or 1-866-331-9474

National Coalition Against Domestic Violence
www.ncadv.org

National Organization for Victim Assistance
www.trynova.org or (800) TRY-NOVA (879-6682)

National Center on Domestic and Sexual Violence
http://ncdsv.org

Americans Overseas Domestic Violence Crisis Center
www.866USwomen.org or 866-USWOMEN (879-6636)

Childhelp USA National Child Abuse Hotline
www.childhelpusa.org or 1-800-4-A-CHILD (4453)

Parents Anonymous
www.parentsanonymous.org or 1-800-421-0353

The Rape, Abuse & Incest National Network
www.rainn.org or 1-800-656-HOPE (4673)

Women's Sexual Abuse Prevention
www.stopitnow.com or 1-888-PREVENT (773-8368)

STD Hotline
1-800-227-8922

Suicide Prevention Lifeline
1-800-273-TALK (8255)

Family Violence Prevention Center
1-800-313-1310

Healing Women Foundation
1-800-477-4111

United Way Crisis Helpline
1-800-233-HELP (4357)

International Mental Health Referral Service
1-800-THERAPIST (843-7274)

Panic Disorder Information Line
1-800-64-PANIC (72642)

OTHER RESOURCES ON SURVIVING AND COPING WITH INFIDELITY

www.infidelity.com
www.marriagebuilders.com
www.survivinginfidelity.com
www.truthaboutdeception.com
www.reafrey.com

APPENDIX B

Extras: Cheat-Sheet Tales

"ABOUT A GIRL"

"Betrayal can only happen if you love."

—JOHN LE CARRÉ (AUTHOR)

I saw her at work at our advertising agency. She was the one everyone noticed, the kind of self-assured woman who would never ask anyone if she looked fat. Strong and confident, she also had a smile that could stop traffic. Emma had an ease about her, an indifference to all the stares or admiring glances. I was drawn to that confidence; it was a trait I would never have.

I was cut from a more sensitive, insecure cloth. I was the woman who changed outfits five times because I sometimes felt fat; the one who would rather stay in on a Friday night with a movie and popcorn than go out to a club. I was the one who would hide in my cubicle rather than stroll through the office smiling and making chitchat with random strangers.

Having been married for five years (but with my husband for about ten), I was a mother of two who worked full-time, hit the gym five days a week, and still made it home in time to cook dinner and have sex with my husband. To say I was exhausted was an understatement. I was reaching a point where my life had become one giant checklist. I wasn't enjoying time with my children or my husband. I was doing just enough to get by, and none of it well. The only solace I found was in church, when I could sit in a wooden pew and listen to someone else talk about what I was supposed to be doing. It was the only time I could believe—*truly believe*—that there was some higher power pulling all the strings.

At night, in bed, I often fantasized about other people. I'd had an indiscretion early in my marriage, with a trainer at the gym. He made me feel strong and sexy, but after a few months, the same insecurities and the same questions returned, and I fled back to the safety of my husband's arms, vowing to love him and only him for the rest of my life. I went to church, I prayed for forgiveness, I worked, I raised our children, and I was back on track for many, many years.

But then I met Emma, and everything changed. Secretly, I had always been curious about being with a woman. Perhaps it was that sensitivity, the idea that I could talk to a woman and she would actually listen, the fact that women smelled good and their bodies were beautiful, and as a mother, sometimes I just wanted another female by my side, and not my gruff, workaholic husband. But, I never pursued it. The rules of the Bible always bubbled up when any of those thoughts crossed my mind (always late at night, always after my husband was asleep), and I would block them before I could imagine myself kissing another woman, feeling instantly guilty—a guilt that would last well into the next day.

My husband and I were having problems. One day, after a particularly bad fight, I was crying in my cubicle when Emma sauntered past. We'd been friendly with each other, as she worked out as well, and we had traded fitness secrets and nutrition tips. She saw my blotched face, my wadded-up Kleenex, my balled fists, and shuddering breaths.

"Are you okay, Liz?"

I looked at her, at those stunning, giant green eyes that still haunt me to this day. "No. Not really. I need a drink, I think."

"Let's get one after work then," she said, as easily as an afterthought. We weren't that type of friends, but the thought of going home to my house and the dishes and my same unmade bed with the tattered sheets literally made me nauseous.

"I'd love to," I said. I called my husband and made sure he could pick up the kids and get them fed. I told him I had a deadline. At a trendy bar downtown, Emma and I sipped wine and I told her everything. How my husband and I had met as teenagers, how he'd rescued me from an abusive relationship, and how I had always felt indebted to him ever since. When he met me, I was broken, pudgy, and unsure of myself. He made me feel beautiful. I lost weight, I got a job, and then I got pregnant: twice. Emma listened, really listened, and at the end of the night gave me a long hug and told me everything would be okay.

"Would you want to come over for my husband's birthday party tomorrow?" I blurted the question before I could even think about it. I just wanted to be near her. "For, for me," I stammered. "It's going to be nothing but guys, and I need some more estrogen in the room."

"Sure," she said. "That sounds . . . fun."

I watched her get into a cab and head to her loft a few miles away. I realized, horrifically, that I hadn't asked her a single question. I didn't know if she was single, married, happy, etc. The mystery about her—that self-assuredness to not have to share or be asked questions—was such an attractive trait. The next day, she brought me a large cup of coffee and a scone.

"Homemade," she winked. "E-mail me your address?"

I nodded, my heart racing. I bit into the scone, a delicious cinnamon buttermilk concoction that I could feel attaching to my thighs with every bite. I pondered what to wear for the party and what food to serve. I dreaded the house full of thirty-something men, rowdy and drunk, stumbling all over my furniture. Would she think my house was a mess? Would she feel sorry for me?

I flew through the rest of the day as quickly as I could and rushed home to prepare. I took extra care shaving my legs, putting on my makeup, and making sure the house was clean. I sent my kids off with the sitter and let my house fill up with men. Right at 8:00 P.M., Emma arrived in skinny jeans, boots, and a top that bared those impossibly toned arms. I could smell her perfume—like sugared almonds—and I gave her a hug as she handed me a bottle of champagne. "Thanks for coming," I said. "And welcome to the zoo."

She fit in perfectly, all the guys falling all over themselves to talk to her, my husband included. I was impressed by the way she melded seamlessly with the boys, the way she nursed her single beer but then switched to water, and the way she helped me in the kitchen, our hands occasionally brushing, and my heart in my throat with every accidental swipe.

Suddenly, my husband was behind me, wrapping his arms around my waist. "I am being abducted," he slurred. I could smell the alcohol on his breath, and immediately, I wanted his hands off of me. Emma's eyes were glued on us, and my cheeks burned.

"Abducted?" I asked, peeling his hands from my hips.

"Yes. Abducted." Jim's friend, Cooper, appeared in the kitchen and draped a long arm around my husband's shoulders. "We're taking him to a strip club. Are you okay with that, Lizzie? We'd ask you to come, but . . ."

"That's funny," Emma interjected. "Liz and I were just about to head out to the strip club too. Male. Hot. *Very* exclusive."

Cooper looked at her approvingly. "Oh, really? Maybe we could all just stay here and *you* could provide the entertainment?"

"Hmm, so tempting, but I left my trashy thong at home. Buh-bye now."

Jim turned to me. "Are you sure you don't mind?"

I shrugged. "No, go. Have fun. Get a lap dance for me." Suddenly, I just wanted them out of my house. All nine of them.

"But I don't want to leave you at home. It's a night without the kids. You should do something."

"I'll keep her entertained," Emma said.

Jim looked at her and then at me. "Are you two going to behave?"

"What?" I exclaimed. "What's that supposed to mean?"

"I promise not to take advantage of her without her *full* consent," Emma joked.

"Okay, good," Jim laughed. "Take pictures," he whispered, before giving me an alcohol-drenched kiss and ducked in the bedroom to change clothes. In ten minutes, the stampede had left, and I poured

Emma a glass of wine and brought her onto the deck. We lived in a neighborhood with lots of trees and were fortunate enough to be close to a lake. I could see the ripple of the water reflected from the moonlight.

"This is so beautiful," Emma murmured. "Such a nice departure from the city."

"Yeah, we love it here," I said. "Listen, thank you for coming. I'm sorry if he embarrassed you at all with that comment. He's a little drunk."

"Not at all," she said. "I don't embarrass easily."

"I wish I had that trait," I said. I took a sip of my wine and savored the warm, red liquid. "So, I'm sorry I didn't ask you a lot of questions the other night. Are you married? Single?"

"Single," she said. "But I'm open to a relationship."

"Well, I'm sure you could have had your pick of the boys tonight."

"Ha. They're not really my . . ."

"Um, *maturity* level?" I joked.

"No, gender," she replied. She looked at me, and I felt my thighs grow moist. "Have you ever been with a woman, Liz?"

"Who? Me? Um, uh . . ." I took a large gulp of wine. A million words shot through my mind. Suddenly, I couldn't remember how to even construct a sentence. I just wanted her to kiss me. "To—to be perfectly honest, I've always thought about it. I've always, you know, wanted to, but just haven't had the, um, opportunity, I guess. And with kids and a husband, I don't think I'm the most attractive candidate."

"You're catnip for most lesbians," Emma laughed. "But trust me, women are a ton of work."

"Have you . . . have you always liked women?"

"Yeah, I have, but I haven't exclusively been with women. I like men actually. I do. They're so simple. You know just what you're getting, and I'm never surprised by them. But to be perfectly honest, having sex with a woman is about the hottest thing on the planet. Nothing feels like that. And kissing a woman . . . those mouths. There are other worlds there."

"Is that so?" I croaked, chugging the rest of my wine.

She shrugged. "I would show you if you weren't married. I find you unbelievably attractive."

I moaned, audibly, and took a step closer, then a step back. Then another step closer, emboldened by the wine and scintillating conversation. I could feel the heat radiating off my body, as I closed the last little gap between us. I looked up at Emma, who was just a few inches taller than I was. Everything in my body ached for her. "Please," I whispered. "Please."

She took my face in her hands, and I closed my eyes. Her lips, feather soft and wet, pressed against mine. Our mouths opened perfectly, our breathing heavy at once. I weaved my hands through her thick hair; I became intoxicated by her scent, by the smooth skin of her neck, by the small, pert breasts pressing against my own, larger ones. Suddenly, she was kissing my neck, then got down on her knees and lifted the lip of my shirt to explore my stomach. I felt my panties grow moist. "Oh my God," I whispered. My thighs pulsed. My entire body was electric. "Fuck me," I heard myself whisper. "Now."

She looked up at me, smiled, and unbuttoned my pants. She stood back up and began kissing me, greedily, and then slid one hand down my panties and pressed me back up against the railing of my deck. She moved her fingers expertly, touching me the exact way I longed to be touched by Jim, but in a way he could somehow never master. Nothing had ever felt so hot. I dragged her inside, removing my pants from my ankles, suddenly ravenous to explore every inch of her body.

We literally could not get enough. I'd once heard a joke about lesbians having sex. How did they know when they were done? Now I understood it; I knew I had experienced something entirely new and singular. After an hour, we collapsed, my heart beating so fast, I began laughing. She was perfect, beautiful in my bed beside me, on the same side Jim slept. Her body was shiny and wet, her cheeks red, her long hair unraveled.

"Perfection," I whispered.

From that moment, I was hooked. I started dressing cuter for work, and Emma and I would slip off whenever we could, fumbling beneath our skirts and panties, in bathroom stalls, in cafés, in parks, wherever I could get my hands on her. I went to her place—often— telling my husband he needed to feed the kids and put them to bed, as I had a huge campaign I was working on. Instead, I was with Emma, falling in love, as I continued to fall steadily out of love with Jim. She never questioned me about my life—we didn't have to discuss the daily grind or how we were going to cut back on the electric bill.

We would make dinner, laugh, curl up and watch movies, give each other massages and have great sex. It was a kind of closeness I had never known with a man, and it was all I wanted. When I got home, oftentimes late, and kissed my children goodnight and stared at their sleeping faces, I felt scared and guilty and unsure of who I was, what I wanted, or what my life would soon become. In church, I felt like crying, like falling to my knees and confessing everything. I prayed, I read Scriptures, I sang hymns, but it wasn't enough to stop me from seeing her.

Jim knew there was a flirtation; he could sense how excited I was to see her, how, if she ever stopped by, I was running around like a child on Christmas.

"Is there anything you need to tell me about the two of you?" he asked one night, as I was preparing dinner for the kids.

"About what?" I asked, slicing a chicken breast into tiny cubes.

"About you and Emma. I'm not an idiot, Liz. You are acting ridiculous."

I scoffed. "Oh yeah, I just forgot to tell you. I'm a lesbian now."

"Are you?"

I shot him a look.

"What? Is that such a crazy assumption? Look at me. Are you?"

I set down the knife and sighed. "Jim, what's this about? What are you getting at? Are you jealous that I finally found a good friend, and my life doesn't revolve around you anymore? I'm allowed to have friends too, you know."

"I never said you weren't," he snapped. "Don't put words in my mouth."

"I'm not putting words in your mouth, but it's not fair. You run off with the boys, go to strip clubs, and grab beers whenever you damn well please, while I'm stuck at home. And do I *ever* give you a hard time? No, never. Well, guess what? Now it's my turn. I *like* Emma. She understands me. She makes me laugh. We have a good time together."

"Well, you two sound like the perfect little couple."

"Don't think I haven't thought about it," I muttered.

"What's that?"

"I said, don't think I haven't thought about it." My face was flaming red. I was sweating. A confession bubbled in my mouth. The words were ready to come spewing out. Should I tell him? Could I?

"Mommy, I'm hungry."

I turned and patted my youngest on her head. "We're ready, sweetheart. Go get your brother."

We ate in silence, and I felt reality come crashing down. I hadn't been able to tell anyone what had been going on for the last three months. I had become sleepless when I wasn't with her. I became so desperate to see her, I would sneak her into my house when Jim worked the late shift, and we would ravage each other, while my children slept upstairs. I was neglecting my family. I told Emma about my guilt, and she understood. She was levelheaded; so much so that sometimes I worried that she couldn't possibly care for me the way I cared for her. But, she supported me.

I had dreams: dreams of leaving the agency, of leaving my family, of returning to painting, something I'd loved to do before I had kids. Emma would sit across from me and let me talk about how hard being a mother was while pouring me a glass of wine and massaging my feet. She constantly made me laugh. And most importantly, she was my friend, my equal.

"You have to deal with all of this," she told me. "You have to figure out what you really want. Is it Jim? Is it your marriage? If it is, save it. This isn't the way to get out of it. You still have to face reality. You can't just run away."

"But *you're* my reality," I whispered, breathing in her neck, her arms, her hair. I knew she was right, though. I knew that the love had gone out of my marriage. Not just the spark or the passion, but the respect and the love. Could we get that back? Did I want to?

The way we talked to each other and moved around each other in quiet, defensive circles was not love. The way he accused me and my constant betrayal wasn't love. The way I snapped at him, the way I literally started to cringe as he touched me wasn't love. We stopped having sex, and I began to pick fights with him just so I could storm out and be with Emma. I'm not exactly sure when he knew I was in love with her, but he knew. I brought her up in conversation all the time, I made plans with her any second I could. I would have sex with her and come home smelling like her, intoxicated by that scent, and he would immediately know where I'd been. I thought because she was a woman, it wasn't really an affair.

Dumbly, I wrote about her. I wrote e-mails, I wrote poems, I texted her all the time. My husband started to check my phone bill, and he even broke into my e-mail account and collected all the evidence. He actually printed out the files, circled all the calls on the phone bill, and told me he would use it against me in court. He started threatening to take my kids away, telling me I was a disgusting human being and God hated me.

But I was so emotionally involved. . . . I was lost. I was so in love with her. I'm not even sure love captures what it was I *felt* for this woman.

Jim finally gave me an ultimatum after seven months. "Either stop seeing her or I'm filing for divorce and I'm taking the kids away."

"You can't do that," I spat.

"Oh, really? *Really*, Liz? Who's the one breaking the law? Who's the one making a mockery of her religion? Of her family? I think I am in a better position than you are. *I* haven't done anything wrong. You have."

As he continued to spew out his venom, I knew I didn't want my marriage; I knew it would never work. He was so angry. I think he had always been angry, and I had been too grateful and too naive to see it. He was already retaliating, having dumb girls call our house and showing up late, drunk and reeking of perfume. I wasn't jealous. I should have been. I just felt tired and slightly envious that Emma's life had been left so perfectly intact, while mine was falling apart.

I wanted a divorce. I told Emma that while we were trying to figure things out, we shouldn't talk. The ease in which she stopped seeing me crushed me. Ironically, she'd received a promotion a month before and moved departments, so I never saw her. I missed my friend, I missed her lips, I missed her laughter, I missed her love, I missed her hands, and I missed our life. But, I had to focus on cleaning up the mess I made. Jim slept on the couch. We barely communicated, and after two weeks of not talking, and almost a year of half-assed trying, of massive fights and bitter words, I filed for divorce. I wasted so much time, when I knew all along it wasn't going to work. He stopped being a good father in the process. He stopped caring completely. My affair changed who he was as a husband, a man, and a father.

If I had just been smarter, if I had never let him know what was happening, perhaps I could have saved us both from that heartache. And it wasn't even *about* Emma: I was using her as a crutch to overlook what wasn't working in my marriage, which never works. I ignored all the signs that I was unhappy. I'm not justifying it, but my husband worked eighty-hour work weeks. We had become roommates. Everything was all about the kids. If I had just taken a step back and realized how unhappy I was, perhaps I could have tried to fix my marriage first before trying to find the attention somewhere else. The simple fact is, we weren't compatible. We had grown apart and were staying together because of the kids.

Once we filed for divorce, I called Emma. By then, months had passed, months in which our passionate nights had become the only memories I clung to. "I am officially separated," I whispered. "I miss you so much." I waited for her to respond, to tell me to come over, to take me in her arms and never let me go.

Instead, she said, "I'm so proud of you, Liz. You took such a big step."

I waited for her to say more. "Um, and?" I probed.

"And I think you have a long road ahead of you. You have to mourn the loss of your relationship and get back on your feet. Figure out what to do next."

"And are you going to be there to help me?" My voice was bordering on hysterical. The thought of her—of all that we'd built, of all that I'd sacrificed over this past year—was one of the only things getting me through. Her and my children.

"Liz, if it's meant to be, it will be. But you need some time alone, I think. To get yourself together and figure out what you really want. I don't want to be a rebound or a mistake."

"Are you serious?" Tears began to fall; giant tears that led to loud, unstoppable wails. I had never cried like this in front of her. "Are you seeing someone else?" I screamed. "Has all of this meant *nothing* to you?"

She didn't respond. I hung up, enraged, lost, so upset by her response that I literally felt reckless. If I couldn't have her, nothing mattered. But, I believed in us, I believed in God, and I knew that if it was meant to be, it would be. It had to. I didn't go through all of that for nothing.

So, I didn't contact her. I sold my house. I went to court. I let the whole messy ordeal unfold as it did, spanning the course of six long months. By that time, Emma had transferred to another agency entirely. She swore it wasn't because of me, but I knew that it was. I missed her on a daily basis. She was the first and last thing I thought about. And time—everyone's nemesis—never made it easier.

And then, two weeks before Christmas, I was in a coffee shop on my way to work, ordering my usual nonfat cappuccino, when I felt a tap on my shoulder. I turned, and there she was—statuesque, fitter than ever, cruelly beautiful. She enveloped me in a hug; a real hug that crushed me to her body before I could speak.

"I thought you had fallen off the face of the planet," I managed. Thankfully, I had a meeting that morning, and was dressed in a black pantsuit. I had lost weight—a lot of weight—and just had my hair died chestnut.

"You look absolutely beautiful," she said. "How are you?"

I straightened. "Good. I'm great, actually. Officially single. Living in a new apartment. Joint custody, so I actually have some time to myself again. I'm taking painting classes actually. So, life is pretty good. And you?" I couldn't believe our casual conversation. Her hands and mouth had been on the most intimate parts of me. She'd tied me up, traced my entire body with her fingertips, and made me have eleven orgasms in a row. *Life is pretty good. And you?* Those casual statements made a mockery of us, of me. I wanted to slap her, to kiss her, to fuck her right there in front of the impatient barista.

"Doing great. I've wanted to call you, but I thought it best you have some time for yourself."

"Yeah, well." I handed over the cash to the barista and moved out of the way for the next customer. "I've definitely had a lot of time."

"Can you sit for a sec?"

She took me to a table and we sat, making small talk. She sat with her hands in her lap. I could tell she was nervous. "I . . . I have something to tell you," she said.

"What's that?" I asked. A promotion? Moving out of the state? God forbid, a *girlfriend*?

"I'm getting married."

I literally felt the world stop. The ground tilted up to meet me. My face flushed. I began to sweat. I felt bile at the back of my throat.

"I wanted to tell you, Liz. I did. It's fast and everything, but you just know when you know. God, I sound like a cliché." She laughed, softly, and I knew that after that day, I would never see her again.

I got up from the table, the world dimming, leaving my coffee and her and everything to step out into the freezing street. I caught myself on a patch of ice and steadied myself, tears streaming down my cheeks. *How?* How could she be getting married? After everything? Was this my karma? Was this my punishment for cheating?

Almost a year later, I am still single, still confused, and still searching. I'm not sure if I could ever be with another woman—it was too intense, too emotional. But, it was so beautiful, so intoxicating, so unparalleled, that it's hard for me to believe that God would send me to Hell for doing something that I felt with my whole heart. I still miss Emma to this day. In many ways, she saved me from myself.

Looking back, I should have asked myself some hard questions about my marriage. I should have prevented myself from going through the motions, and while my affair was what had to happen to make me take the final step in ending my marriage, it has left me with irreparable damage. I am tied to Jim forever. He will always be bitter, and I will always resent the way things ended.

I will spend the rest of my life trying to forget Emma; trying to forget what we almost had, what I wanted, and the lengths I was willing to go to get there.

"IT ALL BEGINS WITH A KISS"

"A hard man is good to find."

—MAE WEST

The ride over to her house was exciting. The mix of anticipation and cold air created a brisk feeling to everything. January in southwestern Ohio was predictable and boring. The holidays were over. A new semester was starting. However, this Friday night was going to be different.

We stopped on the way to Sarah's house to pick up my best friend, Kevin. He hurried to the car and quickly shut the door, so as not to let out any more heat than he had to.

I noticed something shiny and reflective in his hands as he approached the car. I knew right away it was aluminum foil, which could only mean one thing: a hostess gift.

Fuck, I didn't even *think* about the need for a hostess gift! But, then again, were thirteen-year-old boys even *supposed* to know about hostess gifts? I demanded my parents stop at the Kroger grocery. I was not going to go to my first upperclassmen party empty-handed.

We had been to several, if not all, of the freshmen parties. We considered ourselves active in the social scene, but this was different. This would be juniors and seniors, and I was not going to take the chance of showing up without a party gift.

The detour was quick. I bought the old Midwest standby, a cheese ball. Then, it was back in the car. As we pulled up to the house, it was oddly quiet. I knew instantly we should have waited until later to head to the party, as it appeared we were the first ones to arrive. But, my mom had to be home before *Dallas* started. So, inevitably, we were the first two at the party—a party that obviously hadn't yet begun.

The one rule my mom had was that parents always had to be home. It was an understandable rule, and the drill was always the same.

"Parents on the porch," she would say. "The parents *have* to be on the porch."

I had discussed this request with Sarah the night she invited me. It was an awkward exchange, really. I guess juniors and seniors didn't really have to worry about the "parents on the porch" rule. But, as we turned into the cul-de-sac, there was her mom, standing on the porch, just as requested.

The light was dim and several large trees obstructed the view, but I remember thinking her mom looked quite young. Nonetheless I was off, cheese ball in hand, to my first real party.

I didn't know what was louder, the crunch of the frozen ground under my feet or my heart pounding in my ears. I normally was not the nervous type, but I wanted to get everything right. As we got closer to the front porch, I realized why Sarah's mom looked so young—it was her sister. She hadn't come out for my mom's benefit; she heard the car and thought we were her date.

"Sarah's inside. She's still getting ready," she said dismissively, with an obvious disregard for the two young teens standing before her.

Sarah lived on the other side of Cincinnati, in the suburbs. I never really understood why anyone would want to live in the suburbs. Your house was going to look like every other house. A fact I was reminded of only minutes earlier while we were trying to find the right address. Then I walked through the front door and remembered why people *would* live in the suburbs: sunken living rooms.

A sunken living room was something you could only get in the suburbs. The area of the city I lived in was built a long time before this ingenious invention. Regardless, there we sat, alone in the sunken living room, waiting for the rest of the party to arrive.

It seemed like a long time, but finally Sarah made her entrance. I liked Sarah. She was odd, but she was always extremely nice to me. From the first time we met, she would always say hello and ask how my day was going. She never spoke in a full, loud, clear voice. It was always husky and whispered. She blamed it on a bad larynx or trachea or something. I always assumed she did it for attention, just to be different. But, since I had a strange infatuation with Marilyn Monroe, I didn't mind one bit. In fact, I found it oddly amusing, maybe even interesting.

Sarah made her entrance in true style. She never just entered a room. She almost spun into it. It was dramatic, it was big, and it stopped halfway through as her eyes locked on Kevin.

It was at that moment I realized I had never really asked if I could bring him. I had just assumed she knew I would. We were always together. He was my best friend. I wouldn't have even thought about having the balls to show up at this party without my wingman.

She should have known. It was obvious she didn't.

She was nice, nonetheless. Kevin and Sarah were friends as well. We were all in the theater department together, and it wasn't like they didn't know each other. Hugs, hostess gifts, and the pouring of sodas all happened without much incident.

After a few minutes, Kevin was the first to ask. "So, where is everyone?"

It was through quick snippets of conversation only teenagers can have that the real evening unfolded. Sarah's parents: not home. Sarah's sister: leaving. Sarah's party: not really happening.

"What?"

"The party's not happening."

I didn't know who was more disappointed, me, because my first real party wasn't going to happen, or Sarah, because I didn't think her attempt to trick me into coming over was cool.

Either way, there the three of us stood in the kitchen, refilling sodas. None of us sure what to say. I suggested a movie. We returned to the living room, sodas in hand, and the three of us sat on the sofa in the perfectly sunken living room, watching *Dirty Dancing*, of all things. I couldn't stop thinking about the party. How great I knew it was going to be. How funny everyone was going to think I was. How this was my ticket *in*. How many people could have fit into this sunken living room. My mind wandered as I tried to decide if I had misunderstood or been tricked.

Did she say, "I am having a get together," or, "Hey, let's get together!" Either way, it didn't matter. It was disappointing, to say the least.

Then, there was Kevin. I was never going to live—

What was that?

—this down. I mean, he—

There it was again.

It was Sarah. She was blowing in my ear. I must admit the next few minutes were somewhat of a blur. I didn't know if that was because my hormones started to rage, or if my mind had chosen the path of selective amnesia to protect me from the harmful memories. Either way, this was what happened to the best of my recollection.

"Come with me," she whispered in a hushed voice.

"Huh?"

"Come on."

I pointed to Kevin.

"Come *on*," she insisted. She tugged on my arm.

I readjusted the front of my pants and looked at Kevin helplessly. Suddenly, I was climbing steps and kissing Sarah. The door closed, and we were pitched in darkness.

We were alone in her bedroom. It was a nice bedroom. We didn't actually lie on the bed, because it was covered in stuffed animals and dolls. An ironic fact that skipped my thirteen-year-old mind at the time, but now seems somewhat sad.

So there I was on the floor, trying to hide the fact this was the first time I had ever kissed someone. The next few minutes progressed as expected, with kissing, fondling, and heavy breathing.

The heavy breathing was really more for effect, I think. I didn't know why either one of us would be breathing heavy; it really wasn't much of a workout. I was breathing heavy just because she was. I was convinced she was breathing heavy because of the movies she liked.

There was the obvious struggle to try to get the bra undone. The thrust of her hand down my pants. The desire I felt in every part of my body to try this. Then the realization of Kevin sitting down in that beautiful sunken living room all alone.

I stopped.

"What?" she asked, with more husk than I had ever heard in her voice before.

I couldn't even answer. I just stood up. I had to stop. It wasn't right, the whole thing just wasn't right. So I did what I thought best. I readjusted my pants as best I could and headed back down the steps. When I got to the living room, there Kevin sat with the television off, his coat in hand. He was waiting to go home from his first real party. I felt like shit.

He just looked up at me and tried an unconvincing smile. A painful, awkward smile. I asked if he was ready to go, and he said yes. Then, there was a long, cumbersome silence that I will never forget. In that silence, I realized three things:

First, that I was gay; a fact that would take years for me to come to terms with. Second, my best friend was in love with me, a feeling that was mutual. And finally, I had just cheated, a fact that would never allow things to progress for us, and a valuable lesson I would always remember.

Over a decade later, I saw Kevin. I recognized him instantly from across the room. I could tell he recognized me as well but was refusing to relinquish his doubt.

I loved this restaurant. Since moving back to Cincinnati, Fire had to be one of my favorites. The owners had mastered that difficult mix of busy yet relaxing, cool yet understated and did it all with the best bowl of Tom Yum Gai in the city.

Marshall loved Fire as well. We made it a regular habit to go out to eat every Friday. Like most couples, life (i.e., monotony) had gotten severely in the way of what we thought "life" was going to be. Schedules, requirements, restrictions, limits, and expectations had all become the norm, and the carefree spirit that made us fall in love had somehow gotten lost in that list. Friday night dinner, however, was our last bastion of hope. We clung to it and made it a priority. The last priority we seemed to share those days.

Once I gave Kevin a reassuring smile, he made his way across the room rather quickly. I think his arms opened for a hug well before he arrived at our table. I remember noting for the first time how short he was. Even though I knew it wasn't true, I couldn't help but feel that I had grown taller while he had chosen to be happy with where he was as a child. The hug was filled with memories. In that moment I could feel the years melt away as if I was instantly reconnecting with a small part of my soul.

In true Kevin fashion, he was eating alone. His desire and content to spend time by himself was something I never really understood but secretly envied. I was never one who was comfortable being alone. My first reaction was to ask him to join us. His response was a quick "yes." Marshall's was a long sigh.

The conversation was so easy that night. I guess that is always true when you reconnect with someone you haven't seen in a while, but especially true when you were once inseparable. We walked down memory lane. We caught each other up on what had been going on during the second half of our twenties. He brought a new energy to me that night. He reminded me of many things I loved about myself but had forgotten. I wondered how we ever let time slip between us.

As the door of the restaurant opened, we spilled into the street and said our goodbyes. I distinctively remember being hit in the face with a harsh autumn wind. "I love the fall" is a statement many people make because of the changing leaves and their beauty. I personally love fall for other reasons. It feels complex and complicated.

Melancholy is my favorite emotion and nothing is as melancholy as a cool autumn evening. Our bodies, though still warm and tired from the hot summer, welcome the cooler weather, recognizing an end. Not just the end of a season but of so much more.

Nothing could have been truer for me that particular fall. Fall has always been a transitional time for me. All major changes in my life seemed to happen during the fall. I often joked that summer's potential was paid for by the fall. I met Marshall in the fall.

I also met Marshall about the same time I met myself. I say this because unlike many of my friends, "discovering" or "admitting" that I was gay was something that took many years for me to come to terms with. Though I had realized it that night with Kevin, so many years ago, I hadn't acted on it.

However, like most things in life, timing is everything. Within weeks of facing my own personal truth, I met Marshall. It was the greatest moment of my life. I knew instantly that I had to talk to him. Within minutes, I could have told him I loved him. It was perfect, almost silly. What started out as a simple conversation had grown into five years of ups and downs, good and bad, and staying together through thick and thin.

We had so much potential. We came out together, we were each other's first gay relationship, and we learned how to be a couple. The pressure of these factors converged to where we stood five years later. A place I never wanted to be. A place I never saw coming.

The walk home from the restaurant that night was full of conversation. Kevin had barely driven off when Marshall proclaimed, "That was interesting." I wasn't sure how to respond because although I agreed the night had been unplanned and unexpected, *interesting* didn't seem to be the correct word. We would spend the next six blocks trying to decipher what the other meant and what underlying message could be drawn. This is how we had spent the last couple of months. That is what is odd about the end of a relationship; everything that used to be special becomes tainted. I am a firm believer that relationships end long before either person wants to acknowledge it. Our relationship was no different.

I was barely out of bed the next day when my phone rang. I worked from home, so mornings were a luxury I preferred to enjoy uninterrupted. This was a fact that Kevin was not privy to. Regardless, seeing his name pop up was well worth breaking the rules. We would spend the next couple of hours talking and continuing our catch-up session. He claimed he had forgotten to ask me something and that was why he called so soon, but I knew better than that because I had spent the morning searching for a reason to call him too.

Kevin would soon fill the void that existed in my life. We had known each other since we were kids, so time spent together was easy. It was almost like dating without any pressure or expectations —a fact that would make it difficult to share our time with Marshall. Kevin would often tell me that I would make a great boyfriend, and I would just remind him that I already *was* a great boyfriend. I didn't know if I was trying to convince him or myself. I knew Marshall was one person who was no longer convinced. He resented Kevin, hated him in fact. Time spent with Kevin meant time away from Marshall. But I was selfish. I needed the attention. I loved the support. Kevin was quick to remind me of how I was supposed to conquer the world while Marshall reminded me I didn't wash my cereal bowl.

It didn't take long for the delicate dance Marshall and I were participating in to fall apart. We began to do very little together and passing in the hallway would bring a sick feeling to my core. I knew he thought I was cheating on him but was too proud or too scared to ask. I had grown angry with him and didn't want to put his mind at ease. This was a mistake. The truth was I spent all of my time with Kevin talking about Marshall and how I didn't want our relationship to end.

That Halloween I coordinated my costume with Kevin—perhaps a small detail, but only to straight people. Halloween is a holiday gay people love. I swear it's because we were forced to spend so much of our time wearing a mask, but it probably has more to do with the joy of making extravagant costumes.

The party was fine, not anything special but something to do. So many things felt that way. I really spent most of the evening wondering what Marshall was doing and why I had even come. I was sad. Kevin and I agreed it was time to leave and decided to change into normal clothes and grab a bite to eat.

If given a choice of dinner, I was always going to pick Fire. I simply loved it. So Fire it was. Walking in, the irony struck me dead in my tracks. There sat Marshall in the same seat we saw Kevin in a few months prior. My mind raced. I wondered if we should just leave. Should I ask Kevin to leave? Would Marshall want to even eat with us? How did I forget it was Friday? The look in Marshall's eyes made it clear. His decision had been made. Suddenly food didn't matter.

Marshall left, and Kevin and I were soon to follow. The car ride was silent. I didn't have anything to say. Kevin's mind was racing as well. I could tell because he was nervous. When he finally did speak, his voice cracked.

"I love you," he mustered. "I mean, I *could* love you; I have always loved you, really. I want to make love to you. I want you to want to say all of this back to me."

I sat there.

"It's over with him, you know."

I just nodded.

"I want you to spend the night with me. Please."

I licked my lips. "I want you to take me home. I have to talk to Marshall."

He just nodded and drove me home. I didn't even tell Kevin goodbye as I walked into our apartment. I wasn't sure if Marshall was even home. I didn't know what I would say to him if he were.

Inside, he was on the couch, his head propped in his hands. Tears flooded the carpet. I was relieved I didn't have to say anything. Being there said it all. Not known for being comfortable with silence, I gestured toward his to-go food and smiled.

"I guess eating didn't seem like a good idea to you either?" I joked.

I caught a glimpse of the smile that made me fall in love. Saying nothing, we went up to bed. We laid there for hours in silence. We held each other so tight, I could barely breathe. Neither one of us could control our tears. It was powerful. It was beautiful. I had never felt so loved.

The next day, we began the painful process of tearing our lives apart and reassembling them as two separately functioning people. That night marked the end of many things, but it did not end our love for each other or our desire to be part of one another's life.

I would spend the next couple of days trying to touch base with Kevin. I wanted to thank him for bringing me home. I wanted to apologize if I had misled him. I wanted him to know I never meant to hurt him. I wanted to thank him for reminding me that I was a "good guy" and wanted to stay that way. I would never get this chance. In fact, he would never speak to me again.

I tried for months to get him to return a phone call or e-mail. I left notes on his door but never was brave enough to knock. I hated to see him slip away, but somehow knew it was best. I know that night broke the bond we shared. In his mind, he had lost. In his mind, I had cheated on him. Again.

To this day, I still love going to Fire . . . but now I go by myself. I even try to sit in that particular seat at the bar. It holds so much for me. I sit there and remind myself how full life is. I sit there and secretly wait for the door to open and for Kevin to walk back in.

"TWO SIDES TO THE CHEATING STORY"

"Love: A temporary insanity curable by marriage."

—AMBROSE BIERCE (AMERICAN JOURNALIST)

We were young when we married, barely twenty and living on dimes. Looking back, I think those times were actually the most exciting. Living paycheck to paycheck, raising a family and building our little love nest was heaven. Though we were young, I was certain about being married and having children. It's what I'd always wanted. Perhaps because I was a child in the fifties, I had old-fashioned principles.

My husband was a landscaper for his father's business, and though he didn't make any money in the beginning, he had a passion for it, and I supported him. During the summers, I loved making us sandwiches and serving ice-cold beers on our little patio for lunch. Ours was a love unparalleled. While many kids our age were going on first dates, we were building a family. I loved playing house, mainly because I was living with my best friend.

Though we had the stressors of money, our love never wavered. It wasn't until we both turned thirty-five that things took a turn for the worse. Fifteen years together, and to me, I still found the newness and love every day. I think my husband did too, though he definitely went in and out of his moody phases. But, as parents to our three children, we were exceptional. Younger than most and more relaxed (while we weren't hippies, we weren't your typical parents either), our children actually enjoyed being around us, and we enjoyed being around them.

When Stan got a job at a new landscaping firm, he started working longer hours. A mutual friend of ours, Barbara, owned the company with her husband and was kind enough to offer Stan a management position. The job culminated in late nights, fat joints, beers, and endless conversation between the four of us. They only had one child, a daughter, but we could still relate to them. It felt good to have nights away from the kids, to kick back and hold my husband's hand and look at the stars.

Barb and Stan's flirtation wasn't something I picked up on right away. In fact, I was oblivious for the better part of eight months until they had a fundraiser for a very wealthy client, and I went, slinking off to get a drink while Barbara and Stan talked business. When I saw her gaze at him when she thought no one was looking, when I saw that single, solitary look—almost pleading, almost sensual—and the way my husband didn't look away, I simply knew they were having an affair. I felt the vomit rise; I wanted to kill her. Strangely not him, but her.

She knew that I was highly insecure; that I had always been sensitive about my looks, even though everyone told me I looked just like Kate Winslet. I brushed off their compliments, perhaps because the only compliments I wanted to hear were from Stan. But, he wasn't the best with telling me I was beautiful. He just assumed I knew I was.

When we got home that night, and the kids were safely in bed, I lit up a joint and asked him to join me on the patio. I waited until he was sufficiently stoned and then told him I had to ask him something. I came right out with my question: "Are you having an affair with Barbara?"

He froze—only for a second—and then immediately relaxed, taking another hit. "What on earth would make you ask that?"

"Because I saw the way she looked at you tonight. Because you spend every single day with her. Because I have a *feeling*. Christ, you see that woman more than you see your own family."

"No, I'm not," he said. "And give me some credit, please. If I were going to cheat on you, it wouldn't be with Barbara."

"Very funny." This made me smile. Barbara was not overly attractive. She was a smoker. She was a little chubby. I relaxed. But, I still wasn't convinced. I'd always had a gut instinct—some people said I bordered on psychic—and it gnawed at me, this hunch. I knew Stan. I knew he wouldn't come clean unless I had proof. So, I went to collect proof. I went to Barbara.

I called and asked her to lunch. She didn't hesitate to say yes. When I saw her, I scrutinized everything about her. Her thin upper lip, her slight mustache, her frizzy hair, her chipped nails. Surely, Stan had not seen this woman naked.

"Barb, I'm going to get right to the point. Are you having an affair with my husband?"

Rather than laugh or tell me I was ridiculous, her eyes immediately welled with tears.

"Oh, Alice," she sobbed. "Alice." She reached for her napkin. "Did he finally tell you? You have no idea how it's been killing me. I swear, we never meant for it to happen, but we're . . . we're *so* in love. I love Stan so much, I don't know what to do."

My mouth fell open—literally, it fell open. I felt like all the air had been wrenched from my body. "What did you just say?" My voice was the softest I'd ever heard it. "So, you *are* having an affair?"

"Wait, what?" Barbara squinted at me. "Didn't Stan tell you?"

"No, he didn't." I clamped my jaw so hard, I thought it might break.

"I'm . . . I'm sorry, Alice. I thought he told you. I thought . . . well, it doesn't matter. What does matter is that it's out in the open now, so we can decide what we need to do."

I stood up. "What are you talking about, what *we* need to do? *You* need to leave my husband alone." I was irate with myself that I wasn't choking her. Or at least cursing. What was wrong with me?

"But we love each other," she said.

I stared at her snot-drenched face.

"You may love him, but Stan most certainly does not love you."

She scoffed. The bitch actually *scoffed*. "He says the only reason he's with you is for the kids, you know."

"You're delusional," I said. I left and felt my first full-blown anxiety attack coming on. My heart started beating so erratically, I thought I might have a heart attack. Could a thirty-five-year old woman *have* a heart attack? I clutched my chest and made my way to the car, screaming and crying all the way there.

Once home, I called Stan at work and told him to come home, that it was an emergency. When he walked through the door, I knew. I knew by the look on his face that he had already talked to Barb.

"I'm sorry," he said. "I'm sorry I didn't tell you. I didn't know how."

"Do you love that—that *person*?" I screamed.

"No. It's not that simple," he said. "She's my friend. We're friends. I just . . . I just got confused."

He spit out his excuses and I listened as my world disintegrated. I immediately thought of the children. I had vowed to never get divorced. My parents told me we would never make it so young, and it seemed now they would be right. I had married a cheater and a liar. How? How did this happen to me? I thought we were different. I thought we were the exception.

The next day, Stan moved out of the house. Of course, the kids were crushed. After endless begging, Stan asked me to come to therapy. But I told him to go fuck himself. And then I went out with my best friend, got drunk, and slept with a mutual friend. It was a good friend of Stan's actually, and it was amazing. I didn't even feel guilty . . . and I didn't stop there. It's like he'd broken something in me. Always doing the right thing, always following the rules—that was me, good old Alice. But, where had that gotten me? Now I was free.

I slept with four men within the span of two months—double the men than I had slept with in my entire life. I had to get STD tested for the first time, and luckily, I was clean. I managed to be a good parent the entire time. Our children never even knew what was going on. But, as the anger wore off, and I realized what I'd done, I agreed to therapy. Quite simply, after time apart, Stan and I both decided we couldn't live without each other. Sure, my trust was shattered, but the fact that I retaliated, that he *let* me retaliate, that he gave me room to do what I had to, that he let me come to my decision on my own terms and didn't push me . . . it's what saved us. He gave me space, space that I needed, space that I'd never had since I was twenty years old.

We went to therapy. I will never forget the look on the therapist's face as he asked what brought us to see him, and we each produced a list—a list that noted all the things we'd done. "Here's what we've both done. We want to know how to fix it."

And from there, we did fix it. In hindsight, I realized we were probably bound for infidelity. We were so young. We were young parents, and the amount of responsibility we felt at just twenty years old was overwhelming.

All those times I was insulted for my husband not telling me I was beautiful went both ways. He wanted to be complimented too. I put my insecurities off on him. He kept his emotions inside. We had both made mistakes, and it took a long time to regain trust. I punished him for longer than I should have, but he hung in there. I could never bring myself to ask him about what Barbara said about him only staying for the children. If there were even a shred of truth to that statement, I think I would have shriveled up and died.

But, now, thirty years later, I know the answer to that question. His affair did not define our relationship. It was a small period of time in our forty-five year marriage. Our affairs were the very thing to save us. It brought us to a place outside of our routines or crazy schedules. It made us face reality and each other, and we have never been closer. Now we talk, we love, we explain our frustrations, we laugh, we take trips, and we are truly each other's best friend. We aren't together because we *have* to be, or for the kids (as they are long since grown). We are together because we greatly enjoy each other's company, and like we told our therapist all those years ago, no matter what, we cannot live without each other. How many people can say that and do that, even after something like an affair?

I can now say without a shadow of a doubt that there's nothing that can break us. Not another person, not sickness, not losing a child, not even death. Sometimes, I think when you face your worst fear and get past it, you become invincible. While I know we still have to make sure we attend to each other's needs and take care of each other, it never feels like work, and for this, we are both so thankful. We are two of the lucky ones.

"THE ULTIMATE WHAT IF" (REA FREY)

"Bigamy is having one wife too many. Monogamy is the same."

—OSCAR WILDE

"Was that love?"

I stare at the only photograph of him that I own, a wrinkled one of us on the beach together, taken years ago. I keep it folded in the journal he bought me, my heartbreak contained in blue and black ink. In the photo, his hands are wrapped around my shoulder, his fingertips fused to my skin. It would be the only summer we would ever share together. Even the vacation was a mockery—him, stealing away from his wife to drive all night to be with my family. For the next few days, he would laugh with my parents, toss football with my brother, and make giant sand mermaids while I sat under an umbrella and watched him—my temporary fill-in boyfriend. My fantasy. My lie. My *secret*.

I fell for my friend in the kind of way I never thought possible. We were extremely close, despite the fact we were both taken. After a couple years of friendship, it only took one night out alone to become something more. Our connection was instantaneous and dangerous—the closest thing to an addiction I have ever known. I felt desperate, unglued, and fragile. I felt kept and yet suddenly free.

We cooked, we shopped, we played, and we started having sleepovers when his wife went out of town. I slept in their guest bed with him, leaving bobby pins on their hardwood floors, my hair scattered across the sheets, spraying my perfume in their guest bathroom after I showered. I left my imprints around their house but I never set foot in their bedroom. I used his wife's dishes, I sat on her chairs, and I studied her clothes, which hung neatly on garment racks, as though she was just a visitor there. I admired the lace, the silk, the belts, and shoes. As he poured us drinks and fired up the grill, I imagined what it might be like to be her: the Mrs. The wife. Not just the imaginary girlfriend.

As the affair progressed, one month turning into six, I decided to move away. "It's the only way I can stop seeing you," I told him. "I'm going."

"Don't," he said. "Please."

"Give me a reason to stay."

"I can't right now . . . not yet."

"Then I'm going." I shoved my belongings into labeled boxes, my resolve melting with every second leading to our goodbye. I moved, but, of course, I returned to visit, using any excuse to hop on the quick hour flight to see him. I would sit in my parents' guest room and just wail, loudly. After hours, I would stumble into the kitchen, hair disheveled, and feel my lips begin to shake.

"I hate seeing you like this," my mother would whisper. "You're not well."

"But I love him so much," I would whine, feeling that grapefruit-sized hole in my chest.

She would shake her head and sigh. "Oh, sweetheart. That's not love."

I would steel myself to her words and go back to wallowing. He was just twenty miles away doing God knows what, and here I was, suffering, pining, *withering* without him. Why didn't he *care?* I stayed up nights, waiting for him to come to me. The times we did spend together (always on his terms and always after his wife was gone on business), I memorized every detail, like a starved child, because I knew how short-lived it would be. I drank him in; I sketched him in my mind. I took photographs and videos. I journaled. I wrote letters. I inhaled, deeply. I memorized sounds and sentences. By the end of our yearlong affair, I was just trying to keep it all together. Every meeting was peppered by my hot tears, my pleas, and the feeling that I literally could not exist without this other person.

I accepted my role as "the other woman," though I became so much more. I became the best friend, the confidante, the wife, the person he wrapped his arms and legs around at night, the sounding board when he would breathe sentiments into my ear: "I am so in love with you." "You amaze me." "I need you." "Don't leave." One time, he looked at me, those large brown eyes narrowing into slits and said: "Why do I feel like I'm the one who's going to end up all alone in this?" And later, after much debate, "Letting you go will be the biggest mistake I ever make."

"Then *don't*, dipshit," I wanted to scream, but I slowly let him drift away. After the affair came the questions. They accosted me at all hours of the night, all seconds of the day. Was I a terrible person? How could I have done that? What did that make me? What if he had left her in time? What if I had stayed? What if I had told his wife? What if I had gotten pregnant? What if I had waited just a little bit longer? What if I'd showed up at his door? What if I'd asked him to choose me? Can we play these games? Dare we? Would it have made a difference anyway? No matter what I did to move on, he was there, still whispering in my ear, still taunting me with that laugh, still interrupting my sleep, still present, despite the fact that I had moved 400 miles away.

"Why would you want to be with someone who lied to his wife? He's not a good guy. He's a *cheater*," people would say.

"He's not just a cheater," I replied. What I really wanted to say was, "And what does that make me?"

But he *was* more than his actions; he was the guy who told me secrets in the dark, who was vulnerable and quiet, who took stupid risks, who was the resurrected painter, the athlete, who kissed me in public, who raked his large thumbs across my cheeks and made me laugh until I couldn't breathe.

Was that love? I think of that four-letter word, of all that it conjures, both good and bad. Of all that it means. The what-ifs go out the window, because I am here, now, and it has all turned out okay. I think back to that time, at all the sacrifices that went unnoticed, at all the pain and decisions I made for what I thought was love. I didn't know much then, but I am learning. . . . I am learning what love is.

"THE ROAD TO HAPPINESS"
(STEPHANY ALEXANDER)

"Success in marriage does not come merely through finding the right mate, but through being the right mate."

—BARNETT R. BRICKNER (RABBI)

Have I ever cheated? Yes, but not on my husband. It was years before while I was living with a former boyfriend, who I was ready to break up with. I waited until later in life to get married, so I was able to learn from the mistakes of my youth before settling down with the man of my dreams. Nevertheless, in my younger, single years, one of my biggest mistakes was that I was not always careful in choosing my partners, nor did I take the time or even care enough to find out whether they were already in a committed relationship. If I had to do it over again, I would have made a few of my decisions differently. Have I ever been a mistress? No. Have I ever had fantasies or dreams about being intimate with another person? Absolutely. I've had some extremely hot dreams about men (and women) I've been attracted to. However, just because I have fantasies doesn't mean I act on them.

I understand why people cheat. They cheat because they are searching for something they feel they don't have. Love, adventure, an ego boost, sexual desire . . . the list goes on. What keeps me from cheating? Respect and love for my partner. I don't want to cause him pain, plain and simple. I want to make him *happy*.

In my younger years (I'm in my forties now), I was a bit of a wild child. I wanted to try everything, and danger and risk simply didn't phase me. Even though most of my life has been filled with long-term relationships lasting three or more years, it was when I was single that I got into the most trouble. In one of my long-term relationships, I actually cheated at the very end of the relationship to end it faster, something I now regret. It didn't take me long to figure out that I don't like one-night stands. Unless you have a couple of cocktails, feeling physically comfortable with a stranger is not always easy. You don't know what he likes, and he doesn't know what you like, or what the boundaries are. For me, having a one-night stand versus having sex with someone you are in love with cannot even compare. It's like wolfing down fast food as opposed to enjoying fine cuisine or your favorite home-cooked meal. They both get the job done, but the experience of a one-night stand just can't compare on an emotional level. In my opinion, the best sexual experiences can only be reached when you connect on an emotional, spiritual, and physical level. When that happens, fireworks go off. Anything less is just second rate and not as satisfying for me. As I have grown older, it has become more about quality than quantity.

I've watched people I know cheat on their partners. I always wonder why they continue to stay in the relationship if they aren't being satisfied any longer. Wouldn't they rather downsize financially and be happy than maintain financial stability and be unhappy? Cheaters almost always give the same main reasons for staying: for the kids, for the money, because they are codependent, or a combination of those three reasons. Marriage can be difficult if you don't marry the right person.

After a string of bad dates, I met my husband through an online dating website. I was never able to meet any men I was interested in at bars, restaurants, or even through work or travel. Then one evening I was Internet surfing as usual, and I browsed through some of the ads at a popular online dating website and happened to see an online profile that had only been up a few days. It had no photo and the most beautifully written words I had ever read. I contacted this mystery man and asked him to e-mail me a handful of photos and found him to be quite handsome. We went on a date, which wasn't exactly love at first sight, but I enjoyed his company enough to accept a second date, which he carefully planned at an outdoor concert, along with a picnic he packed with my favorite foods. He treated me like a princess, holding my hand gently at first, opening my door, and really listening to me. Outside, while sitting on a blanket under the starlit night, listening to music and eating delicious food, it was love at second sight.

We dated a few years before marrying because I still didn't really trust men, including him, but as time passed and our love blossomed, I grew to trust him. He was kind and patient with me. Probably not the kind of guy I thought I was after in my twenties, but exactly the right kind of guy for me as I grew older and learned some hard lessons. As the years have passed, our love has changed and grown, but my new motto is good guys finish first!

People always ask me how my husband and I are able to keep our relationship so happy, and how we affair-proof our relationship. Well, with my husband, it's quite simple because we are so similar. Our personalities just flow easily around each other. We like the same foods, share the same spiritual beliefs and values, have the same education levels, enjoy the same sports, never argue about where we will travel next, and even have the same taste in art, music, and politics. These commonalities make our relationship so much easier and less work than the relationships I have had in the past.

As crazy as this may sound, it's kind of like being in a relationship with myself, but he's a guy.

However, although we don't argue often, we do have our share of disagreements. When things get heated between us we rely on our "time out" rule, which means that the person who seems the most out of control needs to stop everything and take a walk around the block. This brief break to move your body and breathe some fresh air always helps extinguish our arguments.

I also think that because my husband and I have to travel for our careers, the time apart definitely makes our hearts grow fonder. Too much of a good thing almost always turns bad. Even though I love spending time with my husband, if I am around him all the time, day after day, he starts to drive me crazy and I'm sure I drive him crazy too. I think the travel breaks are absolutely necessary so we have a chance to miss each other and get some time alone. As I have gotten older, girls' night out has also become more important to me. There's something about getting together with my girlfriends and getting goofy, laughing, and gabbing up a storm that fulfills an area that my husband can't fill in quite the same way, even though he is my best friend.

So what else do we do to affair-proof our relationship? We have date night once per week no matter what and have done this for years. Sometimes I put on something sexy and we go out; other times we go see a movie or stay in. We might go to a concert, go hiking, skiing, boating, hot springing, or camping with our dogs. It really doesn't matter what we do as long as we spend some quality time together. Even though we are both extremely busy and active people, we still invest a large quantity of time in each other. Unlike many other couples, we don't stay together because of financial obligations, children, status, or because that's what we are "supposed" to do to fit into society. We stay together because we love each other, we love being with each other, and we want to grow old together.

Little tokens of appreciation go a long way as well. I've made my husband memento books, videos of memories together, and he's written me poetry. We give each other coupons for things like "slave for a day" (one of my favorites for "honey-do" items) or "one-hour massage from each other." One time we made a bet and the winner won "wild cards" which the other person could use at any time to grant whatever wish was desired. I used one of my "wild cards" in the heat of an argument once to immediately end our bickering. The wild cards are so much fun. They definitely take our bets to a more enjoyable and intense level of wanting to win.

Why would I want to cheat on someone who is kind to me and loves me? I wouldn't. My husband does nice things for me every day. I can't even count how many times he has brought me breakfast in bed or has made a beautiful meal. I do the cleanup. I go the extra mile to help him stay organized so he is less stressed and in turn happier, which makes me happier also. See how that works? And I love to pamper him. If his skin is dry, I'll rub lotion on him. If his neck is stiff, I'll massage it. If his car is dirty, I'll wash and detail it by hand to surprise him, and so on.

After years of being together, we both emphasize romance on a regular basis in our relationship. We have candlelit dinners that we prepare lovingly together. We take bubble baths together. We cuddle, hold hands, hug and kiss all the time. On our last trip, we went on an eighteen-mile kayak trip together and paddled to a secluded beach that was only accessible by kayak. It was stunningly beautiful with turquoise blue waters, soft golden-colored sand, beautiful, tall green mountains, and no signs of civilization in sight. Our only friends were the sea lions. We showered in the waterfalls, camped in a cave, looked at the stars, and talked into the night about the constellations, the galaxies, and our plan of somehow meeting each other in the next life. We ran around the beach like we were in the movie *The Blue Lagoon*. At sunset, we gathered a bunch of volcanic rock and created a circle. We stood barefoot in the circle and made up wedding vows to each other, exchanging some twine we tied for rings. We played beautiful meditative music in the background on our iPod. To us, it was absolutely raw and perfect. This simple but unique event meant just as much, if not more to us than any formal wedding or any legal piece of paper could, and I will never forget it.

These are just some of the things we do that not only affair-proof our relationship but bond us closer together. And with a little effort, you can make up your own meaningful rituals that can help affair-proof your relationship too.

Index

"About a Girl" (Cheat-Sheet Tale), 167–82

"Addicted to Adultery" (Cheat-Sheet Tale), 9–10

Adultfriendfinder.com, 103

Adventure, desire for, 146

Affair-proofing, 137–61
  basics of, 138–40
  first-person advice, 208–11
  marriage examination, 140–44
  things to avoid, 144–55
  tips for, 155–59

"The Age of STDs" (Cheat-Sheet Tale), 109–11

Alexander, Stephany, 206–11

Alford, Mimi Beardsley, 18

Alibinetwork.com, 103

Alibis, 4, 37–40, 78

"Alibis Your Partner Might Give If Questioned" (Survival-Guide Tool), 37–40

Allen, Woody, 18

AOL, 86

Appearance, increased attention to, 27–28

Ashleymadison.com, 103

Assets
  online searches, 86–87
  protecting, 76, 126

ATM withdrawals, 4, 26, 82–83

"Bad-Boy Behavior" (Cheat-Sheet Tale), 45–47

"Bad-Boy Red Flags" (Survival-Guide Tool), 47–50

Bad boys, 45–59
  first-person account, 45–47
  questions to ask of, 50–59
  red flags, 47–50

Balzac, Honoré de, 1

"Become Your Own Private PI" (Cheat-Sheet Tale), 65–68

Behavioral clues, 5, 24, 29, 83–85

Benét, Eric, 17

Berry, Halle, 17
Bierce, Ambrose, 195
Bobby pins and rubber bands,
     finding, 6, 7
Boleyn, Anne, 20
Boleyn, Mary, 20
Booty calls, 49–50
Boredom, 95, 144–45
Breaking up
     moving on after, 126–29
     steps to take, 123–25
Brickner, Barnett R., 206
Bullock, Sandra, 17
Buss, David M., 11

Cars
     checking for clues, 27, 83
     GPS installation on, 71, 73,
          77–78, 87
     parking rules of sneaky
          cheaters, 29–30
Cash, 4, 23, 25, 26, 76. *See also*
     ATM withdrawals
Cell phones
     checking records, 7,
          71–72
     GPS installation on, 71, 78,
          80, 87
     passwords on, 25–26, 72
     prepaid, 23
     secret, 71–72
     tracking calls on, 79–80
     tracking services and devices,
          86–87
Cellspyarsenal.com, 87
Chatrooms, 102

"Cheater's Took Kit Exposed"
     (Survival-Guide Tool),
     22–23
Cheating
     caught in the act, 114
     clues to, 3–7
     combination, 15–16
     companion, 15
     emotional (*see* Emotional
          cheaters)
     ending affairs, 30–31
     hiding signs of, 7–8
     most famous male cheaters,
          16–20
     physical (*see* Physical cheaters)
     prevalence of, 10–11
     reasons for (male), 144–55
     rules, 23–32
     serial, 21–22
     shifting attitudes toward, 125
     sneaky cheaters, 22–32
     tool kit, 22–23
"Cheating-Gadget Guide"
     (Uncover), 86–87
Cheat-Sheet Tales
     About a Girl, 167–82
     Addicted to Adultery, 9–10
     The Age of STDs, 109–11
     Bad-Boy Behavior, 45–47
     Become Your Own Private PI,
          65–68
     Confessions of a Personal
          Trainer, 89–91
     A Cyberworld, 99–102
     A Day in the Life of a Serial
          Cheater, 21–22

Falling into Adultery, 1–3
  It All Begins with a Kiss,
    183–94
  It's Not Physical, It's Emotional,
    33–35
  My Wife's Affair, 119–22
  The Road to Happiness,
    206–11
  Two Sides to the Cheating
    Story, 195–201
  The Ultimate What If, 202–5
Cheat-Sheet Tips
  behavioral changes, 85
  legal issues, 88
Checking accounts
  secret, 82
  separate, 156
Children, 68, 74, 116, 123, 126
Chores/housework, 143, 155
Clinton, Bill, 16–17
Cloak-and-dagger syndrome, 68
Clothing
  changes in, 84
  checking, 6, 27–28
Clubmz.com, 87
Co-dependence. *See* Dependence
Codes, secret, 5
Cologne (male), 23, 27–28, 29, 67,
  84. *See also* Scent
Combination cheaters, 15–16
Communication
  importance of, 116–17, 130
  lack of, 153–54
  sneaky cheaters' rules for,
    25–26
Companion cheaters, 15

Compliments, 54–55, 147, 148
Computers. *See also* Online affairs
  asking questions about, 52–53
  checking history and
    documents, 8, 27, 75,
    105
  setting up fake profiles on sites,
    78
  suspicious behavior on, 24, 29
  tracking clues on, 80–82
  tracking software for, 86
Condoms, finding, 7, 8, 23, 25, 27,
  29, 67
"Confessions of a Personal Trainer"
  (Cheat-Sheet Tale), 89–91
Confrontations, 25, 73, 104
  advice for handling, 124–25
  building a case prior to, 74
Counseling, 132
Credit cards, checking statements,
  3–4, 25, 70, 75, 82, 83
Credit reports, checking, 76
"A Cyberworld" (Cheat-Sheet Tale),
  99–102

"A Day in the Life of a Serial
  Cheater" (Cheat-Sheet Tale),
  21–22
Decoys, hidden, 73–74
Defensiveness, 5, 55–56, 158
Dependence, 141, 149, 159
Details left by cheaters, 5–6
Discipline, lack of, 74–75
Divorce, 74. *See also* Breaking up
DNA testing, 87
Duchovny, David, 17

eHarmony.com, 103
E-mail
    checking, 3, 26, 72, 75, 76,
        105, 106
    passwords on, 72
    secret accounts, 86, 103
    sending love letters to partner,
        94
    setting up fake accounts, 78
    tracking clues on, 81
Emotional cheaters, 15, 33–43
    first-person account, 33–35
    preventing affairs by, 41–43
Emotional detachment, 148–49
Entitlement, sense of, 150
E-stealth.com, 87
Excuses, 27, 69–71
Exhaustion, 143
Expectations, unrealistic, 138–39

Facebook, 78, 100–101, 106, 126
"Falling into Adultery" (Cheat-Sheet
    Tale), 1–3
Family, opinions of, 116, 125, 129
Fantasy, 16, 36, 141–42, 157, 160
Farrow, Mia, 18
Fights, handling constructively, 141,
    156, 158
Flirting, 11, 58, 92, 94, 157
Following cheaters, 25, 30
    front-tail tactic, 72–73
    receiving cheater's permission
        for, 31
Forgiveness, 126, 131
Frey, Rea, 202–5

Friends
    cheaters alibied by, 78
    confiding in, 127
    opinions of, 116, 125, 129
    partner's affair with, 113
    spouses/lovers as, 55–56, 130,
        157
Front-tail tactic, 72–73

Gadgets for private investigating,
    86–87
Gas credit cards, 83
Gay couples. See Same-sex affairs
Generosity, 139
Gifts, 25, 76, 82
Giuliani, Rudy, 17–18
Gmail, 81, 86
GPS devices, 71, 73, 77–78, 80, 87
Gym excuse, 69–70

Hairs, checking for, 6, 30
Hanover, Donna, 17–18
Happiness, 123, 137, 150–51
"Happy at Home" (Uncover),
    95–97
Hart, Gary, 31
Healing, 127, 128
Henry VIII, 20
Herpes, 112
Hi5.com, 103
HIV, 112
Hobbies, new, 24, 74, 76
Hockney, David, 33
Home, signs of cheating in, 6–8, 28
Honesty, 132

Hotmail, 71, 86
"How Cheaters Hide Signs of
Cheating" (Uncover), 7–8
"How Do You Know When
You Should Stay Together?"
(Survival-Guide Tool), 133–36
"How Likely Is He to Cheat?"
(Uncover), 59–63
"How to Move on After an Affair"
(Uncover), 125–32
HPV, 112
Hunt, Bonnie, 109

Income tax returns, 82
Infidelitytoday.com, 87
Instant messaging, checking, 7, 106
Instinct, trusting, 23
Intimacy, nurturing, 139, 147
Investigating cheaters. *See* Private
investigating
iPhones, 78, 87, 114
"It All Begins with a Kiss" (Cheat-
Sheet Tale), 183–94
"It's Not Physical, It's Emotional"
(Cheat-Sheet Tale), 33–35

James, Jesse, 17
Jordan, Michael, 19
Journals, 7

Kennedy, John F., 18
Keyghost.com, 80
Key logger software, 80, 86, 105,
107
Knafel, Karla, 19

Landers, Ann, 65
Laughter, 132, 139–40, 155
Laundry, 27–28, 84
Le Carré, John, 167
Legal issues, 26, 88, 114, 116, 126
Leno, Jay, 45
Letterman, David, 18–19
Letters, hidden, 7
Lint rollers, 23, 27
Loneliness, 153
Love
of oneself, 156
rediscovering, 131, 138
Lunch, cheating during, 70–71

Madonna, 119
"A Marriage Examined" (Survival-
Guide Tool), 140–44
Mason, Jackie, 9
Match.com, 103
Meet2cheat.com, 103
Mementos, 6, 7
Meston, Cindy M., 11
Miceli, Lisa, 19
Mobile-spy.com, 87
Money. *See also* Cash
conflicts caused by, 145
following trail of, 3–4, 75–77,
82–83
keeping in perspective, 157
Monroe, Marilyn, 18
"Most Famous Male Cheaters"
(Uncover), 16–20
MSN, 81, 102, 103
"My Wife's Affair" (Cheat-Sheet
Tale), 119–22

Name calling, 48–49, 159
Neglect, 147
Nordegren, Elin, 19

Obsessing, avoidance of, 117
Online affairs, 82, 99–107. *See also*
  Computers
  first-person account, 99–102
  red flags, 104–6
  websites cheaters frequent,
    102–4
"Online Affairs Revealed"
  (Uncover), 104–6
Only You (Hunt), 109
Orkut.com, 103

Paper trails. *See* Money, following
  trail of
Parking rules of sneaky cheaters,
  29–30
Passion.com, 103
Passwords, 25–26, 72, 86
PC Pandora Key Tracking Software,
  86
Perfectmatch.com, 103
Perfume, 3. *See also* Scent
Photos
  hidden, 6, 7, 72
  taken by cheater, 28
  taking, 7, 25, 27, 73, 114
Physical cheaters, 14–15. *See also*
  Serial cheaters; Sex addiction
The Picture of Dorian Gray (Wilde),
  21
Pink (entertainer), 99
Plentyoffish.com, 103

Pornography, 52, 75, 76
"Possible Hidden Clues in the
  Home" (Survival-Guide Tool),
  6–7
Pregnancy, 112, 116
"Prevent Workplace Affairs"
  (Survival-Guide Tool), 91–94
Previn, Soon-Yi, 18
Privacy, increased need for, 24, 53,
  81, 105
Private investigating, 65–88
  first-person account, 65–68
  gadgets for, 86–87
  guide to, 77–79
  instructions for, 68–75
"Quick-Fix Guide" (Uncover),
  115–17
Rcfp.org, 26
Receipts, 6, 75, 76, 82
Recording devices, 26, 30, 77, 114.
  See also Video recordings
Respect, 148, 156
Restraining orders, 113
Retaliation
  foregoing, 127
  by partner's lover, 31–32
Revenge affairs, 148
Riley, Julia, 17
Rmtracking.com, 87
"Roadmap to Prevent an Emotional
  Affair" (Uncover), 41–43
"The Road to Happiness"
  (Alexander/Cheat-Sheet Tale),
  206–11
Rogers, Will, 89
Role-playing guide, 159–60

Romance, desire for, 152
Roommates, feeling like, 154–55

Same-sex affairs
  female, 99–102, 167–82
  male, 183–94
Scent, 3, 27–28, 30, 37
Self-esteem, 127, 130, 146–47
Serial cheaters, 21–22
Sex
  changes in patterns, 5, 24, 29,
    38, 39, 54, 56, 82, 84, 106
  curiosity as reason for cheating,
    152
  importance of, 96, 155
  lack of as reason for cheating,
    151–52, 158
  role-playing guide, 159–60
  safe, sneaky cheaters and, 29
  spicing up, 56, 157, 161
Sex addiction, 9–10, 17, 21–22
Sexually transmitted diseases
  (STDs), 29, 109–11, 112
"Show Me the Money" (Survival-
  Guide Tool), 75–77
SIM cards, 72
Skype, 102, 106
Sleep patterns, changes in, 105
"Sneaky Cheater Rules" (Uncover),
  23–32
Sneaky cheaters, 22–32
  rules, 23–32
  took kit, 22–23
Social media sites, 26, 78, 106
Spycameras.com, 87
Spy cams, 87

STDs. *See* Sexually transmitted
  diseases
"The Step-by-Step Guide to
  Becoming Your Own PI"
  (Survival-Guide Tool), 77–79
Survival-Guide Tools
  Alibis Your Partner Might Give
    If Questioned, 37–40
  Bad-Boy Red Flags, 47–50
  Cheater's Took Kit Exposed,
    22–23
  How Do You Know When You
    Should Stay Together?,
    133–36
  A Marriage Examined, 140–44
  Possible Hidden Clues in the
    Home, 6–7
  Prevent Workplace Affairs,
    91–94
  Show Me the Money, 75–77
  The Step-by-Step Guide to
    Becoming Your Own PI,
    77–79
  Trust Is Tricky, 122–23
  Websites Cheaters Frequent,
    102–4
  What Kind of Cheater Could
    He Be?, 12–16
  Why Men Cheat, 144–55
  Worst-Case Scenarios, 111–14

Telephone calls. *See also* Cell
  phones; Voice mail
  checking records, 39
  decrease in, 48
  evesdropping on, 53–54

Telephone calls—*continued*
   failure to answer, 37, 49, 71
   suspicious behavior during,
      4–5, 24, 53–54, 106
   tracking, 78
   virtual phone numbers, 103
"Ten Ways to Spice Up Your Love
   Life" (Uncover), 161
Text messages, 19–20
   checking, 7, 25–26, 72
   failure to answer, 49
Threats by partner's lover, 113
Thrill of the chase, 149–50
Time, unaccounted-for, 69–71
"Tips for a Cheat-Free Relationship"
   (Uncover), 155–59
Tool kit, cheater's, 22–23
Tracerservices.com, 86–87
Travel
   benefits of, 128
   cheating during, 24–25, 65, 67,
      68–69
"Trust Is Tricky" (Survival-Guide
   Tool), 122–23
"Two Sides to the Cheating Story"
   (Cheat-Sheet Tale), 195–201

"The Ultimate What If" (Frey/
   Cheat-Sheet Tale), 202–5
Uncover
   Cheating-Gadget Guide, 86–87
   Happy at Home, 95–97
   How Cheaters Hide Signs of
      Cheating, 7–8
   How Likely Is He to Cheat?,
      59–63

How to Move on After an
   Affair, 125–32
Most Famous Male Cheaters,
   16–20
Online Affairs Revealed,
   104–6
Quick-Fix Guide, 115–17
Roadmap to Prevent an
   Emotional Affair, 41–43
Sneaky Cheater Rules, 23–32
Ten Ways to Spice Up Your
   Love Life, 161
Tips for a Cheat-Free
   Relationship, 155–59
Ways to Leave Your Partner,
   123–25
Unhappiness, 150–51
Unrealistic expectations, 138–39

Viagra, 75, 84
Video recordings, 28, 73. *See also*
   Recording devices
Violence, 124
Voice mail, 7, 8, 19–20, 78
Volunteering, 128
Von Post, Gunilla, 18

"Ways to Leave Your Partner"
   (Uncover), 123–25
"Websites Cheaters Frequent"
   (Survival-Guide Tool), 102–4
West, Mae, 183
"What Kind of Cheater Could He
   Be?" (Survival-Guide Tool),
   12–16
White, Guy, 68–69, 74–75

"Why Men Cheat" (Survival-Guide
Tool), 144–55
Why Women Have Sex (Buss and
Meston), 11
Wilde, Oscar, 21, 202
Window Washer (program), 80
Woods, Tiger, 19–20, 22
Work
changing habits in, 85
as an excuse, 70
hiding evidence at, 8, 105
spending more time at, 51–52
Workplace affairs, 89–97
first-person account, 89–91
happiness at home *vs.*, 95–97
preventing, 91–94
"Worst-Case Scenarios" (Survival-
Guide Tool), 111–14

Yahoo!, 81, 86, 102

Getting Where Women Really Belong

- Trying to lose the losers you've been dating?
- Striving to find the time to be a doting mother, dedicated employee, and still be a hot piece of you-know-what in the bedroom?
- Been in a comfortable relationship that's becoming, well, too comfortable?

Don't despair! Visit the Jane on Top blog—your new source for information (and commiseration) on all things relationships, sex, and the juggling act that is being a modern gal.